P9-AGA-685

# AMERICA'S DRUG WAR DEBACLE

*I dedicate this book to Fritz Wiedergott, my soccer and lacrosse coach at St. Mark's School, and to Billy Cleary, my ice hockey coach at Harvard University. Their enthusiasm and work ethic inspire me every day to struggle for excellence. I also dedicate the book to my father Andrew Rosenberger and to my mother Wilamena Rosenberger. Their values and support also inspire me to strive for what is right in this world.*

# America's Drug War Debacle

LEIF RODERICK ROSENBERGER
*Professor of Economics*
*U.S. Army War College*
*Carlisle, Pennsylvania*

# Avebury

Aldershot • Brookfield USA • Hong Kong • Singapore • Sydney

WITHDRAWN

© Leif Rosenberger 1996

All rights reserved. No part of this publication may be reproduced, stored in a retrieval system, or transmitted in any form or by any means, electronic, mechanical, photocopying, recording or otherwise without the prior permission of the publisher.

Published by
Avebury
Ashgate Publishing Ltd
Gower House
Croft Road
Aldershot
Hants GU11 3HR
England

Ashgate Publishing Company
Old Post Road
Brookfield
Vermont 05036
USA

ISBN 1 85972 120 6

A CIP catalogue record for this book is available from the British Library

**Library of Congress Catalog Card Number:** 96-84862

Printed in Great Britain by The Ipswich Book Company, Suffolk

# Contents

MAY - 1998

# Acknowledgements

Writing a book like this one is a major undertaking. I certainly could not have written such a book without the encouragement and support I have received from a number of people along the way. First, I want to thank Colonel Jim Gibbons, a former student and a good friend, for helping me to better understand the operational side of the drug war. Second, I want to thank Dr. Gabriel Marcella, Colonel James McCallum, and Colonel Shand Stringham at the Army War College for reviewing drafts of the book and providing me with collegial insight into the Latin American side of the drug war. Third, I owe a debt of gratitude to Joanne Glover and Christine Hockensmith for all of their computer support and to Rita Rummel for her help in formatting the manuscript. Fourth, I'd like to thank Michelle Hughes at Avebury for her confidence in me and her patience, humor and encouragement along the way. Fifth, I want to thank my editor Sarah Brock for her professional advice and encouragement. Sixth, I need to thank all of the impressive people at the White House National Drug Control Office for the time they spent with me and for their insight and expertise. Finally, I need to thank my wife Regina and children Melissa, Emily and Andrew for their patience during the long hours I spent researching this book in the library and writing it in our computer room.

# Preface

As we begin the fourth year of Bill Clinton's Presidency, the President's drug control strategy is in trouble on Capital Hill. His original intent was to begin shifting its emphasis away from reducing the supply of drugs and toward reducing the demand for drugs. Unfortunately, at a time when increasing numbers of middle school and high school students in the United States are using drugs, the U.S. Congress has decided to slash President Clinton's request for drug prevention and treatment.

To be fair to Congress, it is trying to cut all sorts of unnecessary federal government programs in order to eliminate the budget deficit in seven years. This is an excellent economic goal which, if all things were equal, would help long term U.S. economic growth.

But all things are not equal. You cannot have long term economic growth if increasing numbers of Americans entering the work force are struggling with serious drug problems that worsened when Congress cut prevention and treatment programs. You cannot have long term economic growth if we have to divert more and more scarce resources to pay for people with drug overdoses in emergency rooms. If increasing numbers of people are taking drugs, we will need more jails, more prisons, more court time and more police. Where are the savings?

In other words, Congress is ignoring the costly second, third and fourth order effects of cutting prevention and treatment programs. Congress will eventually discover that its well intentioned budget cutting actions contribute to increasing the numbers of Americans saddled with drug problems, which in turn decreases U.S. productivity and U.S. living standards and retards long term economic growth.

As a frustrated Lee Brown passes the baton of Drug Czar to his nominated heir apparent, General Barry McCaffrey, let's hope that the new Drug Czar can persuade Congress to reconsider the errors of its ways and beef up prevention and treatment programs. If so, then a balanced budget might actually happen in seven years thanks to more productive, drug free workers and stronger long term economic growth.

# 1 Introduction

INTRO CONT'

The United States has struggled with drug abuse as a public policy issue for eight decades. It has spent countless billions of dollars on strategies that, at least on paper, mandate a coordinated and balanced attack against drug abuse on the supply and demand fronts. This has included efforts at eradication, interdiction, education, prevention, treatment, and global cooperation. Over the last decade alone the nation's leadership developed and implemented a series of national drug control strategies which spent conservatively, over $76 billion in an effort to make America "drug free."

Despite these well meaning efforts to "win the war on drugs," the insidious cycle of drug abuse and crime continues to be one of the Nation's most serious problems in 1996. Previous progress in reducing casual drug use convinced many Americans that the war was being won. But in many ways, the situation is actually worsening.

Take drug use among America's youth as an example. While the overall number of casual users has been stabilized, rates of illicit drug use are actually rising among the Nation's youth and therefore threatening this Nation's future. More teenagers are using drugs and less of them think drugs are dangerous. Clearly, simplistic "just say no" prevention messages of the past fail to work for today's young people (The White House, February 1995, p. 17).

The war on drugs has also failed to reduce the number of chronic, hard-core drug users. While these hard core drug abusers represent only 20 percent of the drug-using population, they consume about two thirds of the total cocaine in America. These addicted users are also responsible for the preponderance of the crime inextricably linked to the drug problem (1995, pp. 17 and 20).

Some Americans believe they can somehow escape the problems surrounding drug abuse and its social consequences. Nothing could be further from the truth. Drugs are not a problem that impacts only on the poor, minorities or inner city residents. Drug users come from all walks of life and from every corner of America. They are clogging our courts and crowding emergency rooms. On the

1

streets, drug abusers undermine the rights of all Americans to live in a safe environment, free from the fear which the crime-drug cycle creates in our communities.

Even if each and every American is not an actual victim of drug related crime, he or she nonetheless pays a large price for the drug problem. Drugs are arguably undermining the very stability of this Nation and threatening the American way of life in countless ways. For instance, drugs are a huge drain on the overall U.S. economy. In 1993, the retail value of the illicit drug business totalled $50 billion. (1995, p. 11) Second, drugs are weakening the fiscal health of the public sector. Federal, State and local governments spend about $25 billion on drug control efforts, or half of what drug consumers are spending for the illicit drug trade (1995, p. 11).

In the workplace, lost productivity is conclusively linked to drug abuse. Drug users are more likely to be involved in plant accidents and even more likely to file compensation claims. Drug users receive more than the average of sick benefits and are estimated to function at 67 percent of their work potential (Munger and Mendel, 1991, p. 4). The United States is rapidly evolving into a nation that will do more with less and a nation of diminishing resources. We can no longer waste scarce dollars on counter drug initiatives that achieve negligible results. The time is right for an effective national drug strategy. It must begin with an apolitical and unbiased evaluation of past successes and failures. The question is, how can $13.2 billion drug budget successfully challenge an industry that sustains profits of up to $500 billion?

The national drug control strategies have been disproportionately weighted to support supply reduction oriented programs aimed at the eradication of drugs at their source and the interdiction of drugs before they reach U.S. consumers. Nearly 70 percent of the FY92 counter drug funds went into the supply reduction strategy abyss, while only 30 percent was dedicated to demand reduction strategy programs that focused on education, prevention, treatment, and research and development. The latest 1995 strategy requests a FY96 spending split of about 64 percent of the money for reducing the supply of drugs and 36 percent for demand reduction. Given the nature of the problem this is still a lopsided strategy and it is likely to get more lopsided in the years ahead. As of January 1996, Congress seemed determined to cut demand programs to the bone in order to balance the overall U.S. budget. Such budget cutting is penny wise and dollar foolish. Savings from smaller demand side programs will be dwarfed by a spike-up in the spending needed to pay for increased law enforcement and health care costs needed to reach more drug users.

This study will briefly examine the history of America's fight against drug abuse, offering an explanation as to why the country has been so insistent on supply reduction oriented strategies. More importantly, the study will examine the national drug control strategies of the last decade, specifically those under Presidents Reagan and Bush. These strategies will be compared to the more recent

1994 and 1995 drug control strategies proposed by President Clinton. The study will conclude with insights for improving our future programs.

How do we measure success?

Before examining America's early attempts to control drug abuse, it is important to highlight the fact that measuring the effectiveness or success of particular drug control strategies and programs is especially difficult. Statistical data is often lacking and, in almost every instance during research, conflicting data could be found. There are myriad reasons for inaccurate data. For example, it is hard to accurately depict the production, marketing, and profits of the illegal drug industry because of the criminal and clandestine nature of a business which incorporates sophisticated money laundering schemes, shipment networks, etc. (Perl, 1992, p. 30). As Clawson and Lee state in their study, "the best analysts, working with the best techniques and the most accurate information, are unable to agree on the most basic numbers about the cocaine industry" (1992 pp. 2-3). They point out that, although the US Government spends over $13 billion a year fighting drugs, no particular agency has the singular institutional mission to provide overall data about the cocaine industry (p. 5).

On the demand side, it is likewise difficult to precisely calculate the level of drug use. Essentially, there are three major surveys which are used to determine drug use/abuse in the nation, each of which has its own drawbacks and limitations. The National Household Survey on Drug Abuse (NHSDA) has until recently excluded the homeless, the imprisoned, treatment centers, and colleges from its assessments, and it relies on anonymous self-reporting. The High School Senior Survey (HSS) examines only those students present for class and is also self-reporting, although not anonymous. Finally, the Drug Use Forecasting (DUF) is a series of local studies which examine drug use pertinent to specific geographic areas (General Accounting Office, 1993, p. 10). That said, the evidence of increasing drug use among the Nation's youth is persuasive. The debate is over the degree of increase, not the fact that it is occurring. We will explore this question in more detail in the next chapter.

## References

Clawson, Patrick and Rensselear, Lee, (1992), *The Negative Economic, Political and Social Effects of Cocaine in Latin America*, ONDCP Study.

General Accounting Office (GAO) Report, (1993), "Drug Use Measurements."

MacDonald, Scott B. and Bruce Zagaris, (1992), *International Handbook on Drug Control*, Greenwood Press, Westport.

Munger, Merl D. and William D. Mendel, (1991), *Campaign Planning and the Drug War*, Strategic Studies Institute, U.S. Army War College, Carlisle Barracks.

Perl, Raphael F., (1992), "United States Andean Drug Policy: Background and

Issues for Decisionmakers," *Journal of Inter-American Studies and World Affairs*, Vol. 34, Fall.

Smith, Peter, (1992), *Drug Policy in the Americas,* Westview Press, Boulder.

U.S. Army War College, (1993), Department of National Security and Strategy, *Readings in War, National Policy, and Strategy*, Carlisle Barracks, Vol. IV.

White House, (1994), *National Drug Control Strategy*, February.

Wisotsky, Steven, (1986), *Breaking the Impasse in the War on Drugs*, Greenwood Press, New York.

# 2  The Drug Threat

The most alarming trends as mentioned in the previous chapter are the increase in adolescent drug use and the changes in the attitudes of the Nation's youth about the dangers of illicit drug use and the acceptability of such use. Some of the data on these trends comes from the 1994 Monitoring the Future (MTF) study, which offers disturbing information on drug use attitudes and behavior by U.S. students in the 8th, 10th, and 12th grades (White House 1995, p. 20).

The MTF study, for instance, reports a consistent deterioration in attitudes about and perceptions of risks associated with drug use. Eighth and 12th grade U.S. students reported statistically significant declines in their perceived harmfulness of marijuana and LSD. Trends in student disapproval of drug use also showed a troubling deterioration. Similarly, a trend toward more adolescent drug use reported in a 1992 MTF study continues to be reflected in the 1994 MTF study. The 1994 study reports that lifetime, annual, and 30 day prevalence of drug use increased between 1993 and 1994 for the 8th, 10th, and 12th grade students (1995, p. 20)

The Office of National Drug Control states that these upsurges in illicit drug use among the Nation's youth are connected to their use of alcohol and tobacco. The data for this assertion about alcohol and tobacco being "gateway drugs" for adolescents comes from a study done at the Center on Addiction and Substance Abuse at Columbia University.

The Columbia study shows a connection between America's youth smoking tobacco cigarettes and drinking alcohol and their subsequent smoking of marijuana. It also found a relationship between adolescent use of cigarettes, alcohol, and marijuana and their subsequent use of such drugs as cocaine and heroin. For instance, eighty-nine percent of the youth who tried cocaine previously used alcohol, tobacco or marijuana. Similarly, adolescents who used the gateway drugs (alcohol, tobacco, and marijuana) were 266 times more likely to use cocaine than were youth who had never used a gateway drug (1995, p. 23).

The gateway phenomenon may help explain the increasing drug use by adolescents. This upsurge in drug use by America's youth may also be contributing to a possible turning point in overall drug use across America in 1993. The National Household Survey on Drug Abuse (NHSDA) found evidence that the number of Americans using illicit drugs declined from 22.3 million in 1985 to 11.7 million users in 1993. Unfortunately, this general decline has ended and the trend has reversed itself (1995, p. 19).

No significant declines in drug use were reported in 1993 compared to 1992. In other words, current drug use stabilized in America during 1993. And given the gateway phenomenon and the upsurge in adolescent drug use today, an overall increase in the number of Americans using drugs will continue to increase in the future unless the United States changes the way it thinks about and deals with the drug problem. But before we turn to what to do about the drug problem, perhaps it would be useful to have a clearer sense of the drugs we are concerned about.

## Cocaine

Despite all of the efforts to curtail the supply of cocaine in America, there has been no significant reduction in the use or availability of cocaine in recent years. The Office of National Drug Control Policy's most recent Pulse Check for the quarter ending December 1994 reports cocaine use and availability have continued at the same rate in most areas of the United States. Cocaine — especially crack cocaine — continues to be in high demand throughout America. And in some parts of the United States, cocaine use is reported to be on the rise (White House 1995, p. 19).

What accounts for cocaine's continued popularity? One reason seems to be that the dangers of cocaine are misunderstood by the Nation's youth, notwithstanding the well meaning efforts of the people involved in America's embattled prevention and education programs. As cited earlier, the 1994 MTF study reports a deterioration in youth attitudes about the perceptions of risk associated with cocaine. This is particularly true among eighth grade US. students, who reported statistically significant declines in the perceived harmfulness of cocaine powder and crack-cocaine use. For whatever reason, the anti-cocaine message is losing its potency. Although the dangers associated with cocaine use were discovered during the drug's first wave of popularity a century ago, these dangers were largely forgotten or disregarded when the drug resurfaced in the 1960s. In fact, a number of common misconceptions arose over cocaine use.

As recently as the mid-1970s, cocaine was commonly assumed to be harmless and benign. The cocaine epidemic with all its hazards was allegedly scare tactics or media hype. Indeed, it was viewed by many as the ideal "recreational drug." In fact, Cocaine is one of the most insidious drugs on the illicit market, bringing with it the risk of severe physical and psychiatric problems. This is especially true when cocaine is inhaled as "crack." The threat of instant death is always a possibility (NIDA 1988, pp. 18-21).

6

Daily or binge users of cocaine experience extreme changes in their personalities:

> They become "coked out:' confused, anxious and depressed. They become short-tempered, and suspicious of friends, loved ones and co-workers. Their thinking is impaired; they have difficulty concentrating and remembering things. They experience weakness and lassitude. Their work and other responsibilities fall into neglect. Some become aggressive, some experience panic attacks (p. 20).

In extreme cases where consumption is frequent or the dose is particularly high, a cocaine user may experience a partial or total break from reality or cocaine psychosis. The cocaine psychotic has delusions and may become paranoid, sometimes reacting with violence against those he imagines are persecuting him. Many have visual, auditory or tactile hallucination. Cocaine psychosis can continue for days, weeks or months. Severe cases require hospitalization and the use of antipsychotic medications (p. 21).

While these personality shifts are the first visible symptoms, prolonged cocaine use has a significant impact on the body as well as the mind. Neurologic damage due to cocaine use is highly likely. The drug can also injure cerebral arteries which may lead to seizures or epilepsy. Heavy use may cause irregular heartbeats and induce a heart attack. Hypertension, another side effect, can cause a blood vessel in the brain to rupture and cause a stroke. And, finally, a cocaine overdose can kill its user. Death from cocaine is apparently caused by respiratory paralysis (p. 19).

The threats to newborns whose mothers used cocaine during their pregnancies are severe. Ill effects form fetal exposure to cocaine include intrauterine growth retardation and subtle neurological abnormalities. In extreme cases, cocaine can cause brain-damaging strokes. In addition, babies exposed to cocaine are more likely to die before birth or to be born prematurely. They tend to be abnormally small for their age at birth and often have smaller than normal heads and brains. They face an increased risk of deformities, including kidney malformation that can lead to life-threatening infections. And finally, fetal exposure to cocaine often produces impairments in the development of the nervous system. These can interfere with the child's ability to learn and interact normally with other people. Research on older, cocaine-exposed children suggests that the neurological problems may later show up as learning disabilities, hyperactivity and difficulty with focusing (Diegmiller, 1989; Toufexis, 1991; "Crack Children," 1990; Brody, 1988).

## Heroin

Another new development is the link between cocaine and a troubling increase in heroin consumption (White House 1995, p. 25) As crack-cocaine users begin to burn out on the drug's stimulating effects during their high, they are turning to heroin to soften the impact of the "crash" that follows their crack-cocaine binge. Authorities report that growing numbers of crack addicts are smoking heroin with crack, a phenomenon known as "chasing the dragon." The appeal of the combination is that it prolongs the high while slowing down the racing feeling of crack and reducing the anxiety, depression and paranoia that would otherwise occur when the crack wears off. While heroin use nationwide is still relatively low, this new cocaine-heroin link is contributing to an upsurge in heroin use and bodes ill for the future.

In the body, heroin acts as a downer, depressing the nervous system. It deadens the sensation of pain. Many users first feel fear. Drowsiness and clouded thinking follow. Chronic heroin users find it difficult, if not impossible, to maintain a job or normal human relationships. Overdose can kill and so can disease from a dirty needle and allergic reactions to dirt-contaminated heroin. As a result, heroin addicts in their twenties face a death rate similar to that of seventy-year-old men.

## Ice and Crack

Another drug that worries authorities is a methamphetamine known as "ice." Ice is as addictive as crack cocaine but far more pernicious. In contrast to the fleeting 20 minute high of crack, an ice "buzz" lasts anywhere from 8 to 24 hours. It produces immediate and intense euphoria and increased alertness in the user. Its side effects are devastating. It produces aggressive behavior, hallucinations, paranoia and even fatal kidney failure. Moreover, the effect of ice on newborns is alarming: nurses say that ice babies have problems even worse than those of crack babies (Lerner, 1989, pp. 37-38).

The ice trail goes back to South Korea, which, along with Taiwan, leads the world in the manufacture and export of the drug. The rapidity with which it has spread to the United States is startling. It took only four years (roughly 1985-1989) for ice to surpass marijuana and cocaine as Hawaii's number one drug problem (pp. 37-38). And federal drug and customs agents have recently made several ice busts in the continental United States.

But sealing the border in an attempt to keep ice out of the continental United States is not really very effective in the long run, because unlike cocaine — which comes from a plant indigenous to the Andes — ice is synthetically produced by amateur chemists in Asia. It is only a matter of time before these chemists move their operations into American kitchens. Amateur chemists can now duplicate almost any over-the-border drug (Strauss, 1989; Klein, 1985; Zing, 1989).

8

Another insidious synthetic drug is an methamphetamine called "crank." Someone with no chemistry skills, working in a kitchen and using legally available equipment and chemicals, can produce vast quantities of crank. Like cocaine, crank stimulates the nervous system and sends a "rush" to the brain. It keeps the user awake, elevates his or her mood and suppresses the appetite. But it can also make a user nervous and irritable and as the high wears off, crank users become paranoid, aggressive and confused.

A common misperception is that methamphetamines like crank are relatively insignificant in terms of the number of users and does not pose a sizable threat. Again, the facts belie this relaxed view. Crank has become by far the drug of choice in Northern California, and the area is what Bogota is to cocaine (Johnson, 1989; Beaty, 1989). In short, even if you could totally seal the border and keep out all "natural" illegal drug trafficking, synthetic drugs would quickly replace them. Clearly, synthetic drugs will be an increasing problem in the future.


## Alcohol and Tobacco

Until now, our discussion has been focused on the dangers that illegal drugs pose to American society. In fact, up until 1991, the White House National Drug Control Strategy ignored the threat that legal drugs pose to Americans. But in 1992, the White House National Drug Strategy included two legal drugs, alcohol and tobacco, as threats to American society (White House, 1992). And rightly so.

On the one hand, alcohol is like any other general anesthetic. It depresses the central nervous system by slowing down the brain's ability to think and to make decisions and judgments. In this sense, it acts like many other illegal drugs. On the other hand, alcohol is different. Adults can legally purchase alcohol in the form of beer, wine, etc.

Americans have always had an ambivalent attitude toward alcohol. Crusades against alcohol have been followed by periods of relaxation or apathy. Mounting public panic over illegal drug addiction has down-graded alcoholism as a national concern. In fact, it has almost made excessive drinking seem frivolously trivial (Soltis, 1974). And the vocabulary of these addictions, liquor and drugs, has reflected this emphasis. Liquor has been respectable; heroin has not. Drunk has been funny, overdose, tragic. Hangover inspired amusement or sympathy; withdrawal terrified. And so it went: bartender versus pusher, tavern versus opium den.

Yet alcoholism has long been a devastating addiction problem in America. Besides their own suffering alcoholics put enormous strains on their families and friends (Alcohol, 1988). Alcoholism is also an extremely costly addiction for the nation to bear. Industrial losses from absences and inefficiency, not to mention violent deaths, including suicides, accidents and homicides associated with alcohol, cost millions of dollars annually.

Of course, a practice of drinking and alcoholism are not the same thing and it is important to understand the difference. A pattern of sensible drinking means days of not drinking at all mixed with days of light drinking. In this way, sensible drinking does not interfere with a person's health, job, education, relationships, or safety. But too often what begins as sensible drinking gradually degenerates into problem drinking in the sense that it interferes with a person's life. When a person uses alcohol as a major way of coping with stress or cannot control how much he or she drinks, then the person has a drinking problem (Addiction Research Foundation, 1991).

Over the years the U.S. Government has channeled significant amounts of financial resources into exploring the effects of alcohol on the body of an alcoholic. Researchers have discovered that drinking large quantities of alcohol over a long period of time can do serious damage to the body: Brain damage, ulcers, liver disease, malnutrition, heart disease, and various cancers are more common among heavy drinkers. People who drink heavily are likely to die younger than people who drink lightly or not at all. Pregnant women who drink risk having babies with birth defects (Addiction Research Foundation, 1991).

Another phenomenon that worries authorities is the "polydrug" problem. The polydrug problem frequently involves mixing alcohol with other legal or illegal drugs. This mixture can be very dangerous. Especially risky is taking a few drinks with other depressant (or "downer") drugs, such as tranquilizers and sleeping pills. The alcohol and other drug boost the effect of each other, and a person unexpectedly may seem very drunk, pass out, go into a coma, or even die. Even common, non-prescription drugs such as antihistamines (for colds and allergies) can make you dopey and clumsy when you take alcohol at the same time. Taking stimulant drugs such as caffeine, cocaine, or amphetamines after drinking a lot of alcohol is not a good idea either. These drugs can trick users into thinking they are sober, when they are really not — they are just more wide awake and more hyper. Researchers now believe that alcohol makes the body absorb the cancer-causing chemicals in tobacco and cannabis more quickly. If you drink and smoke, you may be more likely to get cancer of the mouth, neck, or throat. Some medicines cannot do their job as well if they are mixed with alcohol. Other medicines can interact violently with alcohol, causing side effects such as cramps, vomiting, and headaches (Addiction Research Foundation).

The dangers of tobacco are not ambiguous. On cigarette advertisements and cigarette packages around America, the U.S. Surgeon General warns that "Smoking causes lung cancer, heart disease, emphysema and may complicate pregnancy." Each year the U.S. Public Health Service reviews the scientific literature and reports to Congress on the effects of smoking on health. And each year the report concludes that cigarette smoking is the single most important environmental factor contributing to premature mortality in America. In fact, the American Lung Association states that tobacco claims more lives than illicit drugs, alcohol abuse, homicide, suicide and automobile accidents combined.

And yet, nearly a third of the American adult population still continues to smoke. Why don't people stop? One reason is that smoking cigarettes, or more specifically absorbing the nicotine drug they contain, is extremely addictive. Though fully aware of the dangers of nicotine, many find it extremely difficult to kick the habit. But what is particularly disturbing is the fact that millions of smokers still do not realize (or perhaps don't accept the fact) that smoking is hazardous to their health.

What does the nicotine in tobacco do to the body? Nicotine causes the release of noradrenaline into the blood stream. Any rise in the level of this hormone produces a rapid heart rate and higher blood pressure, which increases the oxygen needs of the heart. If there is already poor coronary blood flow, the risk of a heart attack increases. Perhaps the most important factor is that cigarette smoke increases the level of carbon monoxide, which results in a decreased capacity of the blood to carry oxygen to the tissues. Lack of oxygen has deleterious effects on the metabolism of the body's tissues.

The good news is that the risk of coronary heart disease reverses fairly rapidly when a cigarette smoker quits. In fact, one or two months after a smoker stops, his or her risk of developing coronary heart disease is almost equal to that of a non-smoker. Unfortunately, risk of lung cancer decreases at no such dramatic rate. If a smoker of a pack or more a day for 10 years quits, it may take 15 years for his or her lungs to return to normal.

If the scientific evidence on the dangers of smoking were relatively recent, then this ignorance or denial would be somewhat understandable. But the U.S. Public Health Service report on smoking came out in 1979 and has remained essentially unchanged:

- Smoking a pack of cigarettes a day decreases life expectancy by 6 years; two packs a day decreases life expectancy by more than 8 years.

- One of every seven deaths in the United States is smoking related.

- Smoking accounts for 80% of all lung cancer deaths (and 70% of lung patients die within the first year).

- Smoking is related to 40% of most other cancer deaths.

- Smoking doubles the risk of heart attack and accounts for one third of all heart disease deaths (and heart disease accounts for about half of all deaths in the United States).

- Smoking accounts for about 75% of emphysema deaths (US Public Health Service, 1979)

11

In addition, studies indicate that smokers may be injuring more than themselves when they light up. Involuntary or passive smoking (inhaling smoke secondhand) may cause diseases such as lung cancer in healthy nonsmokers. A number of other recent studies suggest that nonsmoking wives who have husbands who smoke are much more likely to fall victim to lung cancer and heart disease than those whose husbands do not smoke. Moreover, children who have parents that smoke, are more likely to suffer from respiratory infections, colds, bronchitis, pneumonia than children of nonsmokers.

How then should we view alcohol and tobacco? Probably as the 1992 White House National Drug Control Strategy viewed them, as serious threats to Americans (Ehrenreich, 1988). The new strategy is a welcome departure from the old U.S. counter-drug strategy, which viewed one class of illegal substances as a preeminent enemy while the two most dangerous and life-destroying substances are widely advertised in neon in urban America. Certainly, in terms of sheer numbers, alcohol and tobacco kill the most Americans.

Some would still argue that tobacco and alcohol appear to be relatively larger threats today only because overall illegal drug use decreased after 1988. But even as far back as 1985, when illegal drug use was near its apex, alcohol and nicotine killed approximately 150 Americans for every one who succumbed to the effects of heroin, coke or other prohibited substances. According to the National Council on Alcoholism, alcohol and tobacco were implicated in more than half a million deaths in 1985, while illicit substances were found to be factors in only 3,562. The effects of alcohol upon society are phenomenal: 18 million alcoholics in America, 23,000 alcohol related traffic deaths a year and tens of thousands of work related injuries (Lazare, 1989). And if one compares all legal and illegal drugs, cigarettes cause the greatest loss of life over the long term. The Surgeon General estimates 400,000 Americans die a premature death every year because of cigarette smoking (Good, 1994, p. 126)

None of this discussion is meant to "hype" the threat that alcohol or tobacco pose in order to somehow make a case for outlawing them. Nor is this meant to minimize the threat of cocaine, heroin and the other illicit drugs in comparison to alcohol and tobacco. The point is that we need to put the illicit drug threat in perspective. Alcohol and tobacco — the drugs that kill the greatest number of Americans — are legal and will almost certainly stay this way indefinitely. Therefore, the solution to the drug problem is not to make laws tougher or more lenient. People who take drugs do so for behavioral reasons, not legalistic ones. Therefore, we need to ask a more fundamental question — Why do Americans take drugs regardless of their legality. We will address this question in detail in chapter six.

## Marijuana

The use of marijuana by 8th, 10th and 12th grade U.S. students increased significantly between 1993 and 1994, according to the 1994 MTF study. This trend is consistent with the 1991 MTF study that found evidence that attitudes against regular use of marijuana were weakening among the Nation's youth. These trends are troubling since the latest research provides strong evidence that marijuana is indeed a gateway drug to stronger drugs such as heroin and cocaine (White House 1995, p. 20).

But is marijuana or "weed" itself harmful to the user, even if it does not become a gateway drug for each and every user? The National Institute on Drug Abuse (NIDA) recently reported that marijuana use interferes with short term memory, learning and motor skills performance. There also is evidence that regular marijuana smoking harms one's pulmonary function (White House 1995, p. 18). On the other hand, Harvard psychiatrist and drug researcher Norman Zinberg maintains that "light use of marijuana is certainly not as bad for most people physically as alcohol and tobacco" (Gallagher, 1988).

But what about the chronic marijuana user who smokes it over a long period of time? Can there be permanent damage to the individual? Unfortunately, the kind of definitive research that proved the destructive effects of tobacco and alcohol does not exist. While nothing has been proven yet, Zinberg believes that there is new reason to worry that heavy use of marijuana over long periods of time may well be dangerous. This seems especially true for those who appear most at risk such as young people, heart patients and the emotionally unstable (Gallagher).

But what about the short term effects of smoking marijuana? Is NIDA right? Can there be any adverse side effects? Here the evidence is more conclusive. The use of marijuana does produce a number of adverse side effects in the short run. Hours after the sensation of being stoned is over, the drug can still impair psychomotor performance. That means driving, flying or operating machinery can be dangerous because the operator's coordination, visual performance, reaction time and vigilance are reduced. A Californian study showed that a third of the drivers in fatal car crashes had been smoking marijuana. In addition, a recent train crash in America can be traced to an operator under the influence of pot. Short-term memory and learning ability are also curtailed for hours after smoking marijuana. It is possible that some of the complaints that educators have with the listless performance of their students can be traced in part to the delayed effect that marijuana has on student performance. Certainly it decreases one's ability to think, drive a vehicle and work intelligently, at least in the short term (Gallagher).

The unpredictable impact that marijuana has on the user's emotions is another cause for concern. A common misconception is that smoking marijuana makes users mellow and relaxed. While this is true for some, it is also true that for others marijuana can also cause anxiety and hyperactivity. Fear of losing control or losing one's mind can induce paranoia and anxiety (Gallagher). But doctors stress that it can be difficult to distinguish whether a marijuana problem is a symptom or a cause. The problem is that users in trouble often have pre-existing personality or mood disorders which are aggravated by the drug. In those instances when users lose touch with reality, marijuana may simply be activating a latent psychological problem. Marijuana's potential for stirring up the psyche is why those users with pre-existing psychological disorders are particularly vulnerable (Gallagher).

What is it about marijuana that can produce such negative side effects? Doctors are still searching for the answer, but part of the explanation may be that marijuana is not a simple, or even a single, drug. Its wide range of effects on the body and the mind are caused by the more than 400 chemicals of the cannabis sativa plant. So it stands to reason that each of these 400 chemicals can affect people differently, depending on their psychological and physiological makeup. Overall, there remains much uncertainty about just how harmful marijuana is to frequent users. Some people think that marijuana itself may be relatively harmless over the long term. Clearly, not enough research has been done to support this notion. However, the one point on which all those concerned with marijuana would agree is that having so little knowledge of the drug is, in itself, a dangerous thing.

## References

Addiction Research Foundation, (1991), *Facts About Alcohol*, January.

"Alcohol and the Family," (1988), *Newsweek*, January 18.

Beaty, J., (1989), "Tales of the Crank Trade," *Time*, April 24.

Brody, J.E., (1988), "Cocaine: Litany of Fetal Risks Grow," *The New York Times*, September 6.

Callahan, M., (1987), "How Smoking Kills You," *Parent's Magazine*, December.

Diegmueller, K., (1989), "Passing a Legacy of Drug Addiction," *Insight*, September 4:22-23.

Ehrenreich, B., (1988), "Drug Frenzy: Why the War on Drugs Misses the Real Target," *Utne Reader*, March/April: 76-81.

Gallagher, W., (1988), "Marijuana: Is There New Reason to Worry?" *American Health*, March: 92-104.

Goode, E., (1993), *Drugs, Society and Behavior*: 94/95, Dushkin, Guilford, CT.

Johnson, T., (1989), "Crank Capital, USA," *Sacramento News and Review*, August 31.

Klein, J., (1985), "The New Drug They Call Ecstasy," *New York*, May 20.

Lazare, Daniel, (1989), "Drugs "R" Us," *Drugs, Society and Behavior*, p. 7.

Musto, D., (1989), "America's First Cocaine Epidemic," *The Wilson Quarterly*, Summer.

NIDA (National Institute on Drug Abuse) (1990), *Overview of the 1990 National Household Survey on Drug Abuse*, December: 1-13.

"Cocaine: The Consequences of Use," (1988), [excerpt from report by the National

Institute on Drug Abuse], *Consumers Research Magazine*, January: 18-21.

RAND, (1992), "Cocaine: The First Decade," *Drug Policy Research Center Issue Paper*, RB6000. April.

Strauss, A., (1989), "From Crack to Ecstasy," *American Health*, June.

Soltis, A., (1974), "Alcoholism: Still Problem No. 1," *New York Post*, June 22.

Toufexis, A., (1991), "Innocent Victims," *Time*, May 13.

U.S. Public Health Service Report on Smoking (1979).

White House, (1994), *National Drug Control Strategy*, February 4.

Witkin, G., (1989), "The Return of a Deadly Drug Called Horse," *U.S. News and World Report*, August 14.

"Zing! Speed? The Choice of a New Generation," (1989), *SPIN*, July.

# 3  Origins of U.S. Strategy

Though there were laws on the books during colonial times that prohibited public intoxication, the national attitude toward controlling alcohol and other psychoactive drugs was fairly lax until the middle of the nineteenth century. Alcohol was established early on as a fundamental part of life for both colonists and Native Americans. By the late 1700's and early 1800's many settlers consumed it routinely with every meal. They began the day with an "eye opener" and closed it with a "nightcap. "

Similarly, in the second half of the 19th Century addiction to narcotics such as morphine and opium was far more common in America than addiction to heroin is today. Before and after the American Civil War, while alcohol consumption continued, the use of opium based products skyrocketed. In point of fact, many of the now illegal drugs were at one time seen as beneficial.

When morphine was discovered in 1906, for example, it was thought to be a wonder drug. Products laced with opium and morphine were sold over the counter, through the mail, and prescribed regularly by doctors as a cure all to relieve aches, pains, and for quick "pick me up" (Good, 1993, p. 5). And in the 1880's, coca became widely available as a health tonic and a remedy for a wide assortment of medical ills (Justice, 1992, p. 78). Coca Cola was a prime example of such an elixir. After 1898, heroin was used to treat respiratory illness.

Gradually, Americans began to learn about cocaine's potential for causing addiction. America's "first cocaine epidemic" broke out in the mid 1880's and continued for about 35 years. By the turn of the century, America began to wrestle with the question of federal control over cocaine (as well as morphine). At a minimum, most people felt that the federal government should adopt some kind of drug control. But not everyone was in favor of such government action. In fact, doctors who prescribed these drugs and pharmacists who profited from drug sales generally opposed government actions to control drugs (Woods, 1993, p. 41).

The first laws controlling drug use were passed in the last quarter of the 19th century. The first recorded antidrug law was a municipal ordnance passed in San

16

Francisco in 1875 that prohibited opium dens. The first actions taken at the Federal level prohibited importation of opium by Chinese nationals in 1887. Then in 1906, the Pure Food and Drug Act was passed. This landmark legislation required accurate labeling of patent medicines. Heroin, cocaine and other drugs had to be listed on the label. The act also banned interstate shipment of cocaine and placed a limit on the import of coca leaves (Woods, p. 42). Finally, by 1912, nearly every state had laws controlling the distribution of certain drugs (Justice, 1992, pp. 79-80).

On the foreign front, much of the federal antinarcotics legislation before the 1930's supported U.S. efforts to reduce international drug traffic. In this regard, the U.S. Senate ratification of the International Opium Convention in 1913 committed the U.S. to enact laws to suppress the abuse of opium, morphine and cocaine and helped ensure passage of the Harrison Act in 1914 as the cornerstone of U.S. federal antidrug control

It is important to keep in mind that the logical rationale for the laws against drug use were at least open to lively debate. In the words of Michael Gossop, "As with the prohibition of alcohol, the laws prohibiting drugs were passed not so much on the basis of reasoned argument or scientific evidence, but more often as the result of some moral crusade (1993, p. 154)." The origins of the Harrison Act reflect this U.S. moral crusade. At the end of the 19th Century American newspapers began to run lured stories about Oriental crime and debauchery. The center of this menace was said to be the Oriental opium den. Anti- Chinese feeling was translated into a moral crusade against one of the most characteristic habits of this group, opium smoking. Fear and an hysterical hatred of the Chinese and their way of getting high culminated in the Harrison Act.

The Harrison Act made it impossible for hundreds of thousands of opiate addicts to go on obtaining drugs by legal means. The Harrison Act was also America's first federal regulation to restrict the sale of drugs and is the basis of the current prohibition against narcotics. By taxing and regulating the distribution and sale of narcotics, the act marked a totally new approach to the narcotics problem. Proponents of tough laws against drugs sometimes point to the low level of cocaine use after the Harrison Act went into law. For instance, the Harrison Act permitted the sale of cocaine only through prescriptions. It also forbade any trace of cocaine in patent remedies, the most severe restriction on any habit forming drug to date.

But was the Harrison Act the real reason for this decline in cocaine use? Not according to the U.S. Department of Justice. Justice says that "When the Harrison Act became law in 1914 the use of cocaine had largely died out" (Justice, 1992, p. 80). The tremendous public fear of cocaine had decisively reduced demand. Although the press continued to write about Hollywood scandals and underworld practices during the 1920s, cocaine abuse continued to be a minor problem. By 1930 the New York City Mayor's Committee on Drug Addiction was reporting that "during the last 20 years cocaine addiction has ceased to be a problem" (Musto,

p. 45). In fact, cocaine abuse virtually disappeared from the American scene until the 1970s.

Meanwhile, pressure groups were forming to prohibit the sale of alcohol as well. Temperance societies and other pressure groups were appalled both by drinking alcohol as a form of pleasure and by the social ills of some people who drank too much. They saw drinking as a sin and were determined to enforce their morality on all Americans (Gossop, p. 153). In addition, the Anti-Saloon League saw alcohol as un-American and pro-German and worked hard to prevent an alcoholic subversion of the war effort. And so in 1918 the 18th amendment to the constitution was passed making the sale of alcohol illegal.

While the total amount of alcohol consumption did go down during Prohibition (Woods, p. 43), trying to stop the sale of alcohol ultimately created far more problems than it solved. Prohibition was an era of bootlegging, widespread law-breaking and hideous violence. All over America, illegal alcohol was produced and distributed to meet popular demand. The statistics are staggering. During a one-year period during Prohibition, Americans consumed 200 million gallons of malt liquor and 118 million gallons of wine. By 1930 more than half a million Americans had been arrested for drinking offenses and sentenced to a total of more than 33,000 years of imprisonment (Gossup, p. 153). Worst of all, the black market that sprang up to manufacture and supply illegal alcohol was controlled by organized crime. Over 700 gangland slayings took place during Prohibition. But it was not just criminals who flaunted the law. As the most notorious of the mobsters Al Capone once said:

> I make money by supplying a public demand. If I break the law, my customers who number hundreds of the best people in Chicago are as guilty as I am. The only difference between us is that I sell and they buy. Everybody calls me a racketeer. I call myself a businessman. When I sell liquor, it's bootlegging. When my patrons serve it on a silver tray on Lake Shore Drive, it's hospitality" (Gossop, pp. 153-154).

By the late 1920s, public opinion began to turn against Prohibition. In the face of a huge demand for alcohol, the growth of organized crime and the widespread corruption of police officers, it became clear that the Eighteenth Amendment was impossible to enforce. Consequently, in 1933 Congress passed and the states ratified the Twenty-first Amendment which ended America's experiment in prohibition of the sale of alcohol.

But prohibition as a concept did not go away. While it no longer applied to alcohol in America, prohibition still applied to the non-medical use of drugs. And as time went on, the moral crusade against drugs resurfaced in a different form. According to the Justice Department, "throughout the 1920s attitudes of nationalism nativism, fear of anarchy and of communism were tied to regulation

18

of alcohol and drugs as substances undermining national security" (Justice, p. 79). These attitudes carried over into the 1930s, with the U.S. press attributing horrible crimes, supposedly committed under the influence of marijuana, to Mexican farm workers. The U.S. Treasury Department responded to this hysteria, shifting its focus from controlling heroin to controlling to marijuana. The anti-marijuana efforts of the FBN led to the Marijuana Tax Act of 1937, modeled after the earlier Harrison Act, which required a substantial transfer tax for all marijuana transactions (Justice, 1992, p. 81).

The Eighteenth Amendment to the Constitution is a convincing illustration of what can go wrong when well-meaning law makers try to legislate drug use out of existence. We can trace the custom of "getting high" back at least 5000 years to the use of psychoactive drugs years in the Middle East. What should have been the lesson learned from Prohibition? Laws cannot change overnight the habits embedded in over 5,000 years of human culture. The legislators were strong in their moral certainty that alcohol was a bad thing but weak in their psychology. Drug taking should not be regarded merely as trivial fault in one's morality that can be easily corrected.

During World War II, a surge of patriotism seemed to pull Americans together in the fight against Germany and Japan. Despite the fact that a major wartime mobilization of American society meant a relaxation of drug enforcement at home, the use of illegal drugs was very low and cocaine was almost unheard of. Interestingly enough, a somewhat different situation developed overseas, as cigarettes were distributed free to GIs. Similarly, amphetamines were given to soldiers to increase alertness. Following the war, the number of U.S. smokers increased rapidly (Woods, p. 46).

In the 1950s, the demand for drugs remained relatively low. "Beatniks" and a few other fringe groups did experiment with marijuana and hallucinogens. But these groups were a tiny section of American society. In general, drug use was associated with unpatriotic behavior in the 1950s, as it was during World War I. Consequently many experts predicted that the use of illicit drugs was in its "death throes" (p. 46).

Nonetheless, the efforts to use tough laws to keep drug use down continued. During the 1950s two new laws increased federal sanctions for drug violations. In the Boggs Act of 1951 and the Narcotics Control Act of 1956, the severity of criminal penalties for violations of the import/export and internal revenue laws related to narcotics and marijuana were significantly increased. These penalties included both mandatory minimum prison sentences that were later increased and broadened and higher potential fines for violations. These laws also gave the Federal government the lead role in suppressing illegal drug traffic (Justice, p. 79 and Wolf, p. 47).

In the early 1960s, this trend toward tougher drug laws was visible in international institutions as well. For instance, in 1961, the UN adopted the Single Convention on Narcotic Drugs, which established regulatory schedules for illicit drugs. The convention also created quotas limiting production of and export of legal drugs. The signatories, which included the U.S., committed themselves to work cooperately to control these drugs (Justice, p. 81).

During the 1950s and early 1960s, demand for drugs remained relatively low. But would these new laws be effective in keeping the drug abuse under control over the long term? Would the cycle of drug abuse return? If so, what would trigger it? It didn't take long before these kinds of questions were front burner public policy issues. Illicit drug use came roaring back in the mid 1960s notwithstanding the tougher laws that were now on the books. The new illegal drug industry grew out of a U.S. social revolution that stripped away the social stigma associated with drug use. The 1960s saw the birth of a rebellious youth movement whose slogan was "drugs, sex and rock and roll." In the "psychedelic sixties" drugs were so widespread among rebellious youth that one observer later wrote, "If you remember the Sixties you weren't there" (Woods, p. 8). Marijuana, in particular, became fashionable and was America's drug of choice. But the use of hallucinogens like LSD also increased in the mid 1960s (Woods, p. 48).

What was driving this social revolution in America and what was causing this upsurge in drug abuse? The unpopular Vietnam War and the civil unrest at home prompted more and more frustrated Americans to use drugs as an escape from reality. Similarly, in Southeast Asia, increasing numbers of American troops used marijuana and heroin to separate themselves mentally from the horrors of that ugly war. In short, people were demanding drugs for social and psychological reasons. And this huge demand was easily met by the drug suppliers, who in turn made the job of decisive law enforcement virtually impossible.

But stepped-up efforts to restrict the supply of drugs did not mean all efforts had ceased on the demand front. In fact, President Kennedy opened the decade with a strong commitment to mental health and drug treatment. And many in Kennedy's administration began to look at drug abuse as a behavioral as well as a legal problem. In 1963, the President's Commission on Narcotics and Drug Abuse (the Prettyman Commission) called for a larger Federal role in treatment of drug addicts. The Commission prescribed a network of treatment and rehabilitative services. The Community Mental Health Centers Act of 1963 provided the First Federal assistance to non-Federal entities for treatment.

During the Johnson years the administration opted for a few demand side initiatives as well. Under the Narcotics Addict Rehabilitation Act of 1966, Congress specified that "narcotic addiction" was now a mental illness. In doing so, Congress brought about a major shift that paved the way for Federal support of local drug dependence treatment. And, under the Mental Health Act amendments of 1968, funding was provided specifically for local drug dependence treatment (Justice, pp. 81-82).

Unfortunately, these initiatives were simply too small in scope to make much of a dent, given the skyrocketing demand for drugs in the mid 1960s and 1970s. Instead of a major effort to beef up operating capacity on the demand side to cope with the psychedelic sixties, the primary response continued to be one aimed at reducing the supply of drugs. Thus, a number of major drug control laws were enacted during the Johnson era. Under the 1965 Drug Control Amendments, the manufacture and distribution of amphetamines and barbiturates were brought under Federal control. Criminal penalties were also imposed for illegally producing these drugs. To enforce Federal laws against dangerous drugs, the Bureau of Drug Abuse Control was established within the Department of Health, Education and Welfare (HEW). The amendments also enabled the HEW Secretary to add substances to the controlled list. Finally, in 1968 President Johnson's Commission on Law Enforcement and the Administration of Justice (known as the Katzenbach Commission) urged increased spending to regulate the supply of drugs (Justice, pp. 82 and 84).

In the Nixon years America's robust appetite for drugs continued. The decade started up symbolically with the rock festival Woodstock where drugs were everywhere and consumed openly. Nobody using the drugs seemed to care that new laws had just been crafted aimed at curbing the supply. Once again, frustrated Americans turned to drugs as an escape from reality. As Geraldine Woods puts it, "As the Vietnam War becomes increasingly unpopular, student protests spread. The sense that America is out of control grows" (Woods, pp. 50 and 48).

Instead of focusing on the moral breakdown of the country and crafting a holistic societal strategy, legislators took a legalistic and regulatory approach designed to reduce the supply of drugs. New laws in 1970 focused on the leaders of illegal drug enterprises and added forfeiture of their profits to the possible sanctions. In addition, the Controlled Substance Act of 1970 was passed. This act created a federal standard for drug control. For instance, schedule one listed the most dangerous drugs with no approved medical use (such as heroin and LSD) while schedule two listed drugs that could be used in medicine (cocaine, PCP, amphetamines).

This supply side effort predictably failed to sizably reduce the problem. In fact, the number of bad trips and deaths from illegal drugs skyrocketed during this period. Counterculture heroes Lenny Bruce, Janis Joplin, Jim Morrison, Brian Jones and Jimi Hendrix all died from the effects of drug use (p. 48). In response to this kind of human tragedy, Congress held high level hearings to explore demand side issues. The thrust of the testimony called for greater emphasis on treatment, rehabilitation, training, education and research (Justice, p. 84).

In response to these demand side recommendations, the Drug Abuse Office and Treatment Act of 1972 created the National Institute on Drug Abuse (NIDA) and the Special Action Office for Drug Abuse Prevention (SAODAP). NIDA was established to create comprehensive health, education and research programs for the prevention and treatment of drug abuse. The job of SAODAP was to centrally coordinate the various NIDA programs for treatment, prevention and research in ways to reduce demand, all within the Executive Office of the President (Woods, p. 51; Justice, p. 84). The demand focus, particularly through SAODAP policy,

21

was on direct state spending for services to individuals, educational classes for students, and prevention and treatment programs. In all, the Nixon administration devoted $3 billion to anti-drug activities, and most of it was finally being spent more wisely on prevention and treatment (Woods, p. 51 and Justice, p. 84). On the supply side, the Drug Enforcement Administration (DEA) was created in 1973 by combining the Bureau of Narcotics and Dangerous Drugs (BNDD), the Office for Drug Abuse Law Enforcement, and the Office of National Narcotics Intelligence. All Customs Service personnel mainly dealing with drug law enforcement were also transferred to DEA (Justice, p. 84).

But President Nixon was not content with simply trying to get the U.S. house in order when it came to drug abuse. Nixon saw evil Mexican traffickers exporting marijuana into the United States. Somehow, Washington had to develop a strategy to put pressure on Mexico to crack down on marijuana cultivation and trafficking.

After deciding that the source of the marijuana problem was across the border, Nixon ordered his drug fighters to "seal the border." As part of Operation Intercept, U.S. Customs Service agents began subjecting each and every vehicle to a detailed review. Was Operation Intercept successful? Hardly. Operation Intercept was an economic disaster for Mexico. Mexican farm exports to the United States rotted in the sun as border traffic backed up for miles. U.S. tourist dollars dropped by 70 percent. The Mexican government was outraged, and so were merchants on the U.S. side. Mexicans stopped coming across to shop.

Besides the immediate harm that Operation Intercept had on the economies on both sides of the border, it failed to solve anything. The Mexican government gave Washington a face-saving way for the U.S. to retreat. Mexico agreed in principle to crack down on marijuana trade and Washington called off Operation Intercept after less than a month. The Mexican drug suppliers, who had been laying low during the operation, went back into business. Eventually, Washington pressured the Mexican government to begin spraying the herbicide paraquat on marijuana fields. If reducing the supply of drugs in Mexico was the goal, then Washington was relatively successful.

But then the "iron law of drug economics" took over. After the U.S. squeezed drug traffickers in Mexico, Colombia soon filled the vacuum left by the collapse of the Mexican supply. Thereafter, "U.S. success" at interdicting Colombian marijuana simply stimulated U.S. citizens to grow their own marijuana (Collett, p. 8). And while Washington continued to cast blame at Latin American leaders for allowing marijuana production and trafficking, the United States conspicuously failed to eradicate its own marijuana fields at home. In fact, marijuana soon became a billion dollar business in the United States and arguably the leading cash crop. No wonder marijuana-growing countries like Mexico and Colombia found Washington's sanctimonious sermons about marijuana production in Latin America a bit hypocritical. As Merill Collett, a foreign correspondent specializing on the drug war pointed out, "The United States expects Latin America to eliminate drug root and branch while authorities in Arkansas and California cannot even cut down

22

the marijuana plants flourishing in roadside ditches . . . If Congress were to apply to state governments the same standards it uses to judge Foreign governments more than one governor would find his Federal funds in jeopardy" (p. 42).

In fact, a cynical marijuana grower in Mexico might have seen this U.S. double standard on marijuana as Washington conducting a calculated policy of eliminating foreign competition to protect domestic suppliers. A more prevalent Latin view is that it was politically easier for Washington to fight drugs overseas than at home, where there were millions of marijuana consumers (p. 42).

In a broader sense, Operation Intercept represented the first major U.S. attack on Latin American drugs. The ill considered action had a chilling effect on U.S. relations with Latin America for years to come. In Latin eyes, Operation Intercept was an insensitive, self-righteous and patronizing U.S. intervention into their internal affairs. In this sense, the counter-drug action was consistent with a history of U.S. foreign policy interventions in Latin America.

Finally, Operation Intercept set a precedent for decades of future "Yanqui" counter-drug actions (e.g. cocaine wars) against Washington's "little brown brothers" to the south. To justify these incursions into the sovereign territory of Latin countries, Washington continued to play up the foreign origins of drugs. As Merill Collett notes, "This one-sided perspective skewed the focus of U.S. antidrug action. Having decided that the source of the drug problem was overseas, Washington ordered its drug fighters to go to the source. Thus, most of the big battles in the U.S. war on drugs have been fought on Latin American soil" (p. 4).

Meanwhile, this assumption that drugs were basically a Latin American problem was never shared by the Latins themselves. When Washington blamed foreign drug traffickers, Latin leaders blamed U.S. drug consumers. In 1979 then Colombian president Julio Ceasar Turbay Ayala made this distinction clear when he said, "Colombians are not corrupting Americans. You are corrupting us. If you abandon illegal drugs, the traffic will disappear" (p. 4).

But President Nixon was not content with simply applying U.S. muscle regionally. Just as President Nixon, the fervent cold warrior, once wanted to rid the world of communism, the President now launched a global crusade to rid the world of drugs. In 1971 President Nixon declared a "war on drugs." He viewed heroin as the real threat to America and the heroin traffickers in Turkey as the enemy.

In 1971 a Presidential Cabinet Committee for International Narcotic Control (CCINC) was formed to check the illegal flow of narcotics into the U.S. The Foreign Assistance Act of 1971 provided the means to assist countries to control drug production and trafficking. Committee policies and this Act allowed for the suspension of military or economic aid to countries that failed to control production and traffic of controlled substances (Justice, p. 84). In this regard, the Nixon administration reached an agreement with Turkey. U.S. aid was exchanged for government cooperation in reducing opium production. In addition, the Nixon administration provided foreign aid to finance spraying of opium poppy and marijuana cultivation sites with the herbicide paraquat (p. 84).

In the short term, Nixon's foreign strategy experienced some tactical successes. Seizures of heroin rose, the number of acres of poppy cultivation fell, and the amount of heroin on the American streets dwindled. But instead of seeing this development as a small step in what would have to be a long term, holistic strategy, Nixon declared victory in the war on drugs in 1973 (Woods, p. 52). Nixon's victory statement undermined what otherwise was a relatively sound strategy that put the emphasis on demand reduction. First, declaring victory was naive at best. Shortly after Nixon's victory statement, the iron laws of supply and demand for drugs took over. As Geraldine Woods points out:

> The price of heroin skyrocketed, as did crimes to pay for it. Attracted by high prices, enterprising cartels in Iran, Afghanistan and Pakistan (the Golden Crescent of opium or heroin production) and criminals in Southeast Asia (the Golden Triangle of Burma, Laos and Thailand) entered the market. (p. 12).

Second, the metaphor of a "war on drugs" that could be won or lost would resurface in the Reagan years and haunt anyone trying to deal responsibly and seriously with drug abuse in the future. As alluded to earlier, dealing responsibly with drug abuse is totally different than fighting a war. Drug abuse is a condition that affects individuals and the society as a whole. There is no quick fix or technical solution. Overcoming drug abuse requires a long-term adaptive change on the part of the individual who is tempted to use drugs or who becomes hooked. In short, the war analogy raised false expectations among the American people that "the war on drugs" was winnable. Thus, drug abuse is more like a chemical Vietnam that is unwinnable in a military sense.

Third, "the war on drugs" metaphor conditioned too many Americans to believe that the drug problem was primarily overseas. The image of the United States being besieged by foreign drug traffickers and "invaded" by their products would live on in the minds of supply side counter drug warriors in the United States for years to come. The "blame game" would gradually shift from U.S. drug consumers to evil foreign drug suppliers. This perception of a "foreign threat" appealed to Americans yearning for a seemingly simple solution to complex problems. And as policymakers began to see the problem more in terms of a foreign enemy, U.S. policy would shift more to a supply side emphasis. This shift was subtle in the Carter years and radical in the Reagan and Bush years.

Despite Nixon's drug war rhetoric, his administration carried out a relatively balanced demand/supply strategy. This balance could be seen in Nixon's 1973 federal drug control strategy, which remained the foundation of federal policy through President Ford's presidency in the middle 1970s. Generally speaking, budget allocations reflected this balance. A close look at the budget reveals federal expenditures for prevention and treatment efforts actually exceeding those for trafficking control until 1975.

But in 1976 the objectives and expenditures outlined in the federal drug control strategy began to shift. Law enforcement expenditures exceeded those for prevention in fiscal 1976, 1978 and 1979 (Justice, p. 88). Curiously enough, as the Carter administration began to tilt more to a supply side strategy, it also opted to relax the laws on possession of marijuana. The upsurge in arrests of middle class youth combined with the lively scientific debate over the dangers of marijuana generated pressure to reduce the penalties for possessing small amounts of marijuana. In 1977 President Carter endorsed the decriminalization of marijuana, saying that "penalties against possession of the drug should not be more damaging than the drug itself" (Woods, p. 52). While Carter was against legalizing marijuana, he urged Congress to abolish criminal penalties for possessing an ounce of the drug. Ten states agreed with Carter and have decriminalized small amounts of marijuana. These include California, Colorado, Maine, Minnesota, Mississippi, Nebraska, New York, North Carolina, Ohio and Oregon. Alaska decriminalized possession of marijuana in 1975 but recriminalized it in 1990 (p. 107).

At the end of the 1970s, marijuana use was widespread and pervasive. Generally speaking, police in the United States came to the conclusion that tough law enforcement aimed against marijuana use was futile. Consequently, they eased up on marijuana arrests. Of course, with such a lenient attitude in the White House, it became increasingly difficult for U.S. diplomats in Colombia to persuade Bogota to get tough with marijuana traffickers.

Meanwhile, cocaine came roaring back into popularity in the late 1970s and early 1980s. A U.S interagency group says that U.S cocaine consumption had climbed to between 19 and 25 tons by 1978. But by 1984 it had grown to between 71 and 137 tons (or an increase of 700 percent in just six years (Collett, p. 35). Cocaine's comeback was encouraged by rock musicians and movies (*Easy Rider, Superfly*) whose heroes were cocaine dealers. By this time, cocaine's harmful effects had largely been forgotten. The cocaine comeback was particularly pronounced among the middle class yuppies (young, upwardly mobile professionals). Why was this happening again? Did marijuana smokers graduate to coke sniffing?

While some of the suppliers of marijuana shifted to cocaine, there's nothing in the pharmacology of either drug to suggest that marijuana created a need for cocaine. The effects of the two drugs are different. Marijuana enervates while cocaine energizes. But while there is no physiological connection, the drugs are linked socially. As Merrill Collett points out:

The use of both has a common origin in the defiant subculture that encouraged youth to challenge social taboos against the use of narcotics. In the 1960s consumption increased for every illicit drug — LSD, Quaaludes, PCP, barbiturates, inhalants and others. Cocaine rose to popularity on this wave of mass experimentation. (p. 12).

In short, the American demand for drugs became voracious at this time. Why

25

was this happening? Was it what William James called the "moral weightlessness" of modern times? Was it the American "pursuit of happiness" in an otherwise grim period? Whatever the reason, drugs, including alcohol and tobacco, are "thoroughly woven into U.S. life. The government would have to rip apart the social fabric to totally extract illicit drug use from the U.S. national culture" (Collett, p. 54).

While President Carter did not explicitly link drugs and broader societal problems in the United States, he did deliver an important speech in which he said America had lost its sense of moral direction and purpose. America was in a spiritual vacuum, a malaise. Perhaps the sense that America was out of control at the time of Woodstock in 1970 was still true in 1980. Maybe cocaine's comeback was simply a reflection of this broader social demoralization.

How Ronald Reagan would approach the drug control problem was not altogether clear at the time he became President. Some people expected he would take a tough law and order approach and put his emphasis on law enforcement and limiting the supply drugs. Others speculated that since Reagan was an admirer of free market economist Milton Friedman, the new President might possibly agree with Friedman's position that fighting the supply side battle was a losing proposition as long as the demand for drugs was so overwhelming.

Initially at least, Reagan seemed to side with Friedman. At his first press conference in March of 1981, the newly elected president stated he would refocus U.S. antidrug policy on the demand side: "It's far more effective if you take the customers away than if you try to take the drugs away from those who want to be customers" (Collett, p. 24). Unfortunately, Reagan's subsequent actions did not reflect this early rhetoric.

In fact, Reagan did quite the opposite from what he promised in March of 1981. The Reagan administration shifted to a radical supply side strategy. The Reagan administration poured huge amounts of human and financial resources into an unwinnable war to repress drug supply while cutting the funds aimed at reducing drug demand. Federal drug control spending on supply side programs (law enforcement, interdiction, investigation, eradication and international cooperation) had averaged $437 million annually for the preceding five years before Reagan took power. But during the first five years of the Reagan era (1981-1986), spending on these supply side programs more than tripled to an annual average of $1.4 billion. In these same Reagan years, funding for demand side programs of drug treatment, rehabilitation, education and research fell from an average of $386 million a year to $362.8 million (p. 24).

Reagan's shift to a lop-sided supply side strategy was particularly evident if one compared law enforcement spending with spending on drug treatment. In the 1981 drug control budget, law enforcement received about 60% of the federal drug control spending. In contrast, drug treatment only received about half of the money going to law enforcement in 1981. By 1984, the supply side strategy was firmly in place. Reagan's 1984 Crime Control Act provided increased penalties for major drug offenses and gave federal prosecutors new authority to seize assets of drug dealers (Woods, pp. 54-55). The 1984 federal drug control strategy called for $1.2 billion for law enforcement in fiscal year 1985 — the highest in history — compared to only $252.9 million for demand functions (Justice, p. 88).

Although the United States spent most of its money for drug law enforcement on domestic police action, the overall thrust of the anti-drug strategy was aimed abroad, particularly at the cocaine traffickers in Latin America. (See next chapter.) Consequently, before the mid 1960s, Washington tended to paint Americans as helpless victims of evil Latin American traffickers. But in the mid 1980s a number of events forced the United States to abandon this self-delusion and openly acknowledge that it was one half of the drug trade equation (Collett, p. 4).

By 1986 the cocaine situation was getting worse. A much more dangerous crack cocaine (a smokeable form of cocaine) hit the streets with a vengeance, bringing with it a wave of instant deaths and a surge of social destruction in the inner cities. As drug abuse became a political issue in the mid 1980s, U.S. Congressmen challenged Reagan's supply side strategy, which had clearly failed to curb the explosion of cocaine use. As Merrill Collett points out, "Simmering discontent on Capital Hill turned into a full-blown revolt after basketball star Len Bias (first round draft choice for the Boston Celtics) and the Cleveland Brown's defensive back Don Rogers both died of cocaine overdoses in the same month, June 1986" (Collett, p. 30). A national outcry prompted Congress to intervene in and put pressure on the Reagan administration to increase spending on demand side programs. The result was $1.7 billion omnibus drug bill known as the Anti-Drug Abuse Act of 1986. This Act tried to reach into every phase of illegal drug production and consumption.

Unfortunately, only a few demand side initiatives demonstrated indications of "getting smart" on drug abuse. Too many did not focus on why Americans were taking drugs, nor did they provide much help for people trying to get off drugs. Instead, Reagan's demand side strategy emphasized "getting tough" on drugs. In other words, the thrust of it was punitive. It endorsed the use of sanctions aimed at drug users to reduce the demand for drugs. President Reagan called on Americans to mobilize for a national crusade against drugs "to help us create an outspoken intolerance for drug use" (Woods, p. 57).

Reagan's domestic crusade against drugs soon became known as the "zero tolerance" program. Reagan promised to get the users and prosecute them, no matter how small the quantity of the illegal found in their possession. The punitive aspects of this initiative as well as complementary initiatives were contained in Reagan's 1986 Anti-Drug Abuse Act. These included: mobilizing national intolerance to any use of drugs; emphasis on user accountability (Justice, p. 85); an introduction of mandatory urine testing for specific populations and in the workplace. On the demand side, the 1986 Anti-Drug Abuse Act increased treatment and prevention efforts aimed at reduction of drug demand and expanded alcohol and drug treatment and rehabilitation grants to states. It also encouraged greater emphasis on using volunteer and community grass roots efforts and media outreach to reduce drug use. These were all praiseworthy actions. The problem was that these non-punitive demand side actions were minuscule in terms of the overwhelming problem at hand.

By 1986 the gap between law enforcement spending and drug treatment was actually getting wider. Law enforcement received over 70% of the drug control budget in 1986 while drug treatment had fallen to little more than 20% of the budget (or less than 1/3 of the law enforcement figure) (Justice, p. 130). Moreover, the demand side programs as a whole still received a smaller share of the total federal drug control funds than before the Reagan years. Thus, instead of focusing on the origin of the problem, the demand for drugs, the Reaganites remained committed to a futile and expensive law and order approach aimed at cutting off supply (Collett, p. 24).

## References

Collett, M., (1989), *The Cocaine Connection.*

Goode, E., (1993), *Drugs, Society and Behavior.*

Gossop, M., (1993), *Living With Drugs.*

Musto, D., (1994), "A Brief History of American Drug Control," in Goode, E. *Drugs, Society and Behavior.*

U.S. Justice, (1992), "The System: A National Report from the Bureau of Justice Statistics." *Drugs, Crime, and the Justice System: A National Report*, December.

Woods, G., (1993), *Drug Abuse in Society.*

# 4  A Militarized U.S. Strategy

During the Reagan era, the war on drugs became increasingly lop-sided. More and more of the national drug control budget was spent beefing up supply side programs. But the Reagan administration correctly said "just say no" to frequent requests to unleash the U.S. military in this war. Secretary of Defense Weinberger and his successor Frank Carlucci argued long and hard against militarizing the drug war.

But when George Bush became President, drugs skyrocketed to the number one issue in America. Crack cocaine was on the street and parents were frantic. They looked to the President and Congress for a quick fix solution to this frustrating drug problem. New Secretary of Defense Dick Chaney had been a U.S. Congressman and was particularly sensitive to the winds blowing from Capital Hill. To prove to the American people that the new administration was really serious about the war on drugs, Chaney and the Congress opted to get the U.S. military involved directly in the war. They sold the American people on the fiction that the "can do" U.S. military could keep cocaine out of the country by decisively sealing the border.

Never mind that many professional military officers argued that this domestic political objective would be an extravagant and wasteful mission. This military adventure was especially frustrating to the Pentagon, which was seeing its budget for real wars  cut to the bone.


**The Militarization Of The Drug War . . . Is It Cost Effective?**

To some extent, this unprecedented militarization of the drug war is consistent with America's determination during the last decade to eradicate the drug abuse menace. It should be noted early on that increased military involvement was primarily the product of a congressional and public outcry to save America from the drug scourge. The military was, and continues to be in some circles, cautious in its involvement in "winning the war on drugs." (Dilulio, 1993, p. 30).

Military support for the first war on drugs actually began during the tenure of President Nixon. The Pentagon gave small amounts of equipment to help the Coast Guard and Customs Service in their interdiction efforts. However, support was both limited and sporadic (Dickert, 1992, p. 1). The origins of DOD support for the counterdrug effort can be traced back to the Defense Authorization Act of 1981. Prior to this act, the Posse Comitatus Act of 1878 prevented the military from participation in police and domestic law enforcement actions. The military was a strong supporter of the Posse Comitatus Act and throughout the 1980s opposed any changes to the act (p. 2). However, the translation of the Defense Appropriations Act into Public Law 97-86 amended the Posse Comitatus Act and allowed DOD to give limited support to federal agencies. Specifically, the amendment permitted the following: providing information collected during the normal course of military operations; the use of military equipment and facilities; allowing military personnel to operate and maintain that equipment provided; and finally the training and advising of civilian law enforcement (p. 2). The amended Act stopped short of U.S. military personnel participating in search, seizure, and arrest activities. Additionally, it provided two caveats to support: assistance would not interfere with military readiness or preparedness and there would be no direct participation by military forces in interdiction (Trumble, 1991).

However, the war on drugs during the 1980s failed to stop the increasing flow of drugs into America. Once again, Congress called for further measures which would give the military increasing powers to interdict, search, and arrest drug traffickers on the seas. However, throughout this timeframe the military resisted this creep in their mission. Secretary of Defense (SECDEF) Weinberger was vehemently opposed and stated that the military's role violated the tenets of the Weinberger Doctrine which shaped the rationale for military involvement in world affairs. The six criteria for military employment were: a vital national interest is at stake; sufficient forces are committed to win; clearly defined political and military objectives are established; adjustment of forces is permitted once they are committed; reasonable assurance of congressional and public support is expected and military forces are committed only as a last resort (Dickert, p. 4). A strong case can be made that U.S. drug policy fails to meet some, if not all, of these criteria.

Weinberger's successor, SECDEF Frank Carlucci, continued the struggle against DOD involvement in the drug wars. He stated in 1988,

> I remain absolutely opposed to the assignment of a law enforcement mission to the DOD. And I'm even more firmly opposed to any relaxation of the Posse Comitatus restrictions on the use of the military to search, seize and arrest (p. 5).

However, drug abuse soon became America's number one public enemy and the

Congress wanted to show its resolve in the war on drugs. Thus, in 1989 America witnessed the passing of the Defense Authorization Act which tasked DOD with extensive interdiction and counterdrug missions. Specifically, for the first time it made DOD the lead agency for detecting and monitoring the drug flow. (Carlucci, 1988, pp. 256-257). Nevertheless, DOD continued to resist further participation and was accused by Congress in February 1989 of being late in implementing their new mission (Dickert, p. 6). In support of this new mission, President Bush issued his new National Drug Control Strategy on September 5, 1989. It mandated a three-phased concept to fight the war on drugs. Phase one was to attack drugs at their source through 'nation building assistance' and support for host country forces. U.S. forces were authorized to assist foreign nations in training, reconnaissance, command and control, planning, logistics, medical support, and civic action. It also permitted support to host nation police forces (p. 6) Interdiction of drugs from the source country to the United States was phase two of the national strategy. Phase three was to attack drugs domestically. This was accomplished by training civilian law enforcement and providing support in the form of the National Guard (Trumble, p. 15).

Did militarization of the drug war help to reduce drug abuse in America? Unfortunately, the answer is no! That is not to say the military performed poorly from a narrow operational perspective. Indeed, the bulk of eradication and interdiction successes over the last several years have been either directly or indirectly attributable to consistent and professional military support. They have assisted in dismantling cartels, provided sophisticated equipment for detection, communications and surveillance support, and trained thousands of foreign and U.S. law enforcement personnel.

However, other sources tend to be more critical. A recent GAO report cited that nearly $2 billion worth of detection and monitoring equipment over the last two years has had no significant impact in reducing the drug flow. Further, it accused DOD of turf wars with other governmental agencies, (such as the DEA) and of poor management, poor intelligence, policy confusion, and doing lasting damage to Latin American countries that are unstable. (p. 17).

Nevertheless, the Pentagon will continue to support the drug war so long as the American people and Congress mandate such operations. In fact, it is the law. Aside from the tangible results of drug seizures, there are other less tangible from the military's participation in the drug war. First, as any commander will testify, counterdrug operations offer some training. Concurrently, it allows the U.S. military access to host nations and establishes relationships and support infrastructures within a particular nation. Such support is often critical during regional crisis. But on balance, the Pentagon's war on drugs is a bad idea.

Given the current drawdown of military manpower and decreasing budgets, should the military continue to be a major player in the war on drugs? Will there be enough forces to conduct "operations other than war." Or should America's forces be focused on winning two near simultaneous regional conflicts as proposed in a recent Bottoms Up Review of U.S. force structure? These questions are and will remain major points of debate as the nation struggles with foreign policy and balancing the budget.

From a grand strategy perspective, DOD unfortunately has not significantly affected the influx of drugs into America. The inevitable fate of continued DOD support is inextricably linked with force and fiscal drawdowns. Given the current forecast, it is time for the military to cut its losses and reorient towards warfighting and more germane operations other than war, such as tackling the challenge of nuclear non-proliferation and doing what it can in Bosnia to bring peace to this war torn area. In short it's time for the Pentagon to "just say no" to the "war on drugs."

Now that we have addressed why the military mission is so costly and futile, let's take a birds-eye view of the international context for this mission impossible. In this regard, the last decade witnessed a deadly transition of the international drug industry, which in turn posed a more complex calculus to America's decision makers. Scott MacDonald and Bruce Zagaris offer a number of cogent and articulate reasons for this change in the structure of the international drug trade (1992, pp. 7-11).

Take the American desire for cocaine for example. This U.S. appetite for cocaine has increased dramatically over the last decade. In response to this growing demand, Colombian drug traffickers developed a sophisticated network of production, processing, and distribution of the drug. They were also successful neutralizing law enforcement within their country and eliminating competitors. Concurrently, heroin continued as the drug of choice for Western Europe and parts of Asia. In response, some nations such as the Netherlands relaxed their laws and legalized selected aspects of drug use within their countries.

The Soviet invasion of Afghanistan also created fertile grounds for an explosion in opium production and trade. The combination of the overall breakdown of authority in Afghanistan, the expansion of clandestine networks to fight the war, and the Mujahidin's need for capital were decisive contributors to this expanded opium industry.

The Islamic revolution also provided the genesis for the third factor in the changing international drug industry. Iran became a major transport point for illegal drugs and supported opium and heroin production in Lebanon.

In addition, there's been a substantial crackdown on the drug trade in Latin America. The end result, unfortunately, was a more sophisticated network of distribution involving many different routes which made interdiction, at best, a marginally effective tactic.

Another development takes us to the other side of the world. Burma has always been a major producer of opium and the collapse of the Ne Win regime in 1988 saw a concomitant decrease in law enforcement efforts to curb opium production. Therefore, by 1990, Burma was the world's major opium producing country, transporting their product and laundering their money throughout Asia.

The sixth development was the combination of the Colombian crackdown on narco-trafficking in 1989 and the U.S. invasion of Panama. Both events closed down Panama as a transshipment point for drugs and money laundering, which meant a restructuring of transshipment networks, unfortunately expanding the industry into other Latin American nations. Additionally, as the Medellin Cartel declined, the Cali Cartel became the prominent drug organization in Colombia.

The seventh development complements the first point made about America's insatiable appetite for cocaine. The U.S. cocaine market became saturated in the 1990s, and as demand for cocaine leveled off the narco-traffickers sought new markets and product diversification. Europe, Japan, and the Middle East became new consumers for Latin American cocaine.

The surging market for synthetic drugs marks the eighth reason for the changing international drug industry. An explosion of production has occurred across the globe with such nations as the Philippines becoming major producers of methamphetamine. Access to chemicals and a crude laboratory are the essential ingredients for this new type of drug scourge.

The ninth development recognizes the global drug dilemma. Nearly every nation in the world has become either a user, producer, transshipper, money launderer, or all of the above.

In response to the global proliferation of the drug trade, we see a concurrent global governmental response. Although embryonic in scope, this is a positive sign that suggests a multi-lateral and multi-national approach to solving the international problem of drug abuse.

Unfortunately, America's leadership failed to comprehend the significance of the evolving drug trade. More simply put, U.S. leaders failed to "know their enemy" or to comprehend the points outlined above. Instead, they fell back on old failed policies to counter a larger and more complex problem. Militarizing the drug war was simply the most tangible manifestation of these failed policies. Thus, the decade of the 1980s not only saw more of the same, but an intensity, even a fanaticism, on the part of national leadership in combatting drug abuse. Drug budgets soared. International summits were arranged from which strategies were proposed. And as cited earlier, the drug war took on a new face: militarization.

In his October 1982 address to the country regarding drug abuse, President Reagan was supremely optimistic that his administration could unequivocally conquer the drug scourge. Reagan stated," . . . for the very first time, the Federal government is waging a planned, concerted campaign against drugs . . . drugs are bad and we are going after them . . . we've taken down the surrender flag and run up the battle flag . . . and we're going to win the war on drugs." (Zimring and Hawkins, 1992, p. 48). Was he successful? His own "President's Commission on Drug Crime" stated that the crisis had grown nationally and internationally. Also, the Commission stated that drug abuse "still ruins individual lives, drains billions of dollars each year from American society and erodes the nation's quality of life." (p. 47).

One would think that the following administration (Bush) would have adopted a program that was more assured of success. On paper, the strategy proposed by President Bush did seem more expansive and had more inclusions that courted a demand side strategy, but in essence it was more of the same, with increased escalation of supply side initiatives. President Bush's focus was primarily the cocaine industry, and the revised drug war took on a three pronged strategy: force the Andean countries to eradicate coca leaf production, interdict the flow of drugs northward from the Caribbean and Mexico, and intensify the pressure on drug producers and traffickers (p. 47).

## Anti-Drug Bias

To complement this continuum of supply weighted strategies, four major Federal anti-drug bills were enacted during the decade (McCoy and Block, 1992, p. 1). The first Crime Control Act was enacted in 1984 and reflected President Reagan's get tough on drugs message. It expanded criminal and civil asset forfeiture laws, allowing for the seizure of more drug related property incidental to offenses. The Bail Reform Act was also amended to target pretrial retention of defendants accused of serious drug offenses. Overall, Federal penalties for drug offenses were increased. These penalties complemented the establishment of a determinate sentencing system.

The 1986 Anti-Drug Abuse Act not only stiffened some of the measures of the Crime Control Act, but also reflected some interest in demand and domestic oriented strategies. The Act budgeted money for prevention and treatment programs and created a drug law enforcement grant program to assist state and local governments. On the punitive side, it restored mandatory sentences for large scale marijuana distribution, added designer drugs to the list of prohibitive substances, and attempted to strengthen international drug control initiatives.

Two years later, the 1988 Anti-Drug Abuse Act further tightened sanctions and punishment against drug users, traffickers, and international producers. On the demand side, prevention and treatment efforts were increased and for the first time the organization of the Federal drug program was changed in an attempt to facilitate better coordination.

The Crime Control Act of 1990 expanded measures designed to seize drug traffickers' assets. Additionally, it enhanced regulatory procedures for precursor agents. Provisions on money laundering, rural drug enforcement, drug free school zones, and drug paraphernalia were also included in the Act. It doubled the appropriations for law enforcement grants to states and communities. Finally, it expanded drug control and education programs, although not nearly enough to offset the lop-sided supply side strategy.

## So Why Has The Strategy Failed?

Despite this unprecedented surge in legislation, resources and dollars the programs have failed to significantly reduce and control drug abuse in the Nation. Melvyn Levitsky, the Assistant Secretary for International Narcotics Matters, testified before the House Foreign Affairs Committee in 1993, "Hundreds of tons of cocaine still flow into the U.S.; the drug trafficking industry continues to be strong, ruthless, and adaptable; major traffickers continue to exploit the weaknesses of governments beset by societal-economic-political unrest; and drug financed corruption continues to be one of the greatest impediments to counternarcotics efforts" (Justice, 1992, p. 86).

Most of all, the national leadership over the last two decades has not carefully analyzed the scope of the problem to find what Clausewitz calls the center of gravity . . . "the hub of power and movement on which everything depends" (Levitsky, 1993, p. 387). Where should decisive force (resources) be applied to tackle drug abuse? The answer is not simple; the enemy is a goliath. "The drug trade has evolved into a complex, sophisticated, transnational industry, whose growth is fostered by unregulated international markets in chemicals, a transportation revolution, and globalization of banking and financial markets" (Lykke, 1989, p. 3).

Although the national strategies mandate a balanced approach, they allocate the lion's share of too few drug budget dollars to eliminating drugs at their source and interdicting drugs at the borders. There is a synergism between supply and demand strategies that must be recognized and balanced. Even more, the nation is terribly impatient and wants instant results. No strategy will ensure that end state. "There is no quick fix solution, no cost free outcome. Policy makers can only seek least-bad solutions" (Flynn and Grant, 1993). If demand is eliminated or reduced, the problem is well on the way to being managed. Unfortunately, however, it requires the changing of attitudes which is a generational task that does not occur overnight. Education and prevention, over the long term, must be balanced with effective short term reductions in supply as a corollary policy goal (Smith, 1992, p. 15).

## Eradication And Interdiction Tactics

Eradication and interdiction operations have been, and continue to be in modified form, the backbone of our national drug control strategy. Yet they are the toughest equations in the drug problem set, maybe too tough to ever solve. In reading the White House report, National Drug Control Strategy: Progress in the War on Drugs 1989-1992, the naive reader is easily impressed with eradication and interdiction successes. In aggregate, it is true that selected operations and programs have eradicated and interdicted a great deal of drugs. The Office of National Drug

35

Control Policy (ONDCP) uses eradication and interdiction statistics as a measure of success, and from a pure eradication and seizure perspective, thousands of tons of cocaine and other illegal drugs have been eliminated from our streets. This paper will not denigrate these efforts, nor the agencies which executed their counternarcotics jobs. Given their marching orders, these professional men and women have performed admirably.

Unfortunately, when compared to the overall amount of drugs produced and which eventually reach the consumer, these successes are mere grains of sand on the beach. It is like scooping out a quart of water from a gallon bucket. Sure, there are only three quarts left, but that is sufficient to satisfy an individual's daily consumption rate. Can the nation look itself in the mirror and say that it is cost effective in view of the fact that it has not substantially affected demand within America? There are several reasons why the supply oriented strategy is not doing so well, which in turn require further examination.

**Production Proliferation**

Despite massive eradication efforts in Andean countries such as Peru and Bolivia, coca is grown in more places today than ten years ago. An equitable argument can be made for the production of heroin. When law enforcement pressure is applied in one area the growers and traffickers easily shift production to alternate sites. This same lift and shift strategy applies for production labs in such nations as Colombia. Historically, this argument is well supported, as cited earlier. After being pressured by the United States, Colombia in the 1970's took massive steps to reduce its production of marijuana. But the net result was the relocation of the marijuana production industry to Mexico. Once again, under pressure from the United States, the Mexican government started eradication measures and the marijuana crop shifted to the United States. U.S. domestic production now satisfies one third of global demand (Van Wert, 1992, p. 22). In Latin America, specifically Peru, the production of coca has spread from the Upper Huallaga Valley to Cuzco, Ayacucho, Pasco, and Puno areas (Smith, 1992, p. 8). The bottom line is that the U.S. has unknowingly helped to sow the seeds of the production proliferation problem elsewhere in Latin America; "a continent predisposed to seeking narco-dollars by its low per capita income and development prospects and its levels of corruption" (Flynn, 1993, p. 8).

Another adaptation of the drug industry to eradication efforts is the generation of new versions of the same drugs, but with more toxic effects and lower prices. For example, the movement of marijuana away from both Colombia and Mexico resulted in more potent "made in America" strains. Likewise, "crack" reflects efforts by traffickers to reach a larger market (America's urban poor) at a lower price than cocaine (Gene, 1992, p. 16). Kevin Zeese summarizes this well: "Clearly, the destroy it at its source strategy has had many negative repercussions.

36

It created new markets for drugs under attack, created new and more powerful drug lords, encouraged more potent and dangerous drugs, and made it more difficult to control the supply of drugs" (Gene, 1992, p. 9). According to ONDCP officials, the producers now counter the effects of eradication and interdiction not only by making a more pure form of cocaine from a lesser quantity of leaves than before, but also by squeezing more coca paste from the same amount of leaves. This "tit for tat" counter thrust underscores the business nature of drug production and trafficking and the seriousness of the drug lords to continue making profits. There are also arguments that it is too late for further drug strategy in the Andean nations. Some say attention should be focused on new areas of production such as the aggressive drug industry flourishing in Eurasia, or the new production sites in the Ukraine (Zeese, 1991, p. 254).

## Production Alternatives

An integral component of the current eradication program is the "carrot and stick" crop substitution program in which America provides indigenous farmers with incentives to substitute other crops for illegal ones. At the moment, over 600,000 families in Peru are employed directly or indirectly in the drug trade (Lee, 1989), 400,000 people are directly employed in Bolivia with an incalculable number indirectly involved such as lawyers, accountants, bankers, etc (Marcella, 1994). About 1.5 million Colombians, Peruvians, and Bolivians are involved in the cocaine trade (Smith, 1992, p. 10). For many reasons, the crop substitution programs have miserably failed in Latin America. Yet since 1989 over a billion dollars has been spent toward this initiative. First, how can America be so naive as to think that a Peruvian or Bolivian farmer, who makes more in one season growing coca than from several years growing corn, would revert back to his corn crop? How many Americans would voluntarily take a step back financially? It is not that there are insufficient alternative crops out there such as bananas, coffee, etc. In the Upper Huallaga Valley, citrus fruits, bananas, yucca, and a few other selected crops could compete with coca for gross income revenue. Likewise, in the Bolivian Chapare region, macadamia nuts, black pepper, rubber and citrus fruits bring in more revenue than coca (Newsweek, 1990, p. 33). However, according to ONDCP sources, these countries lack a sufficient transportation and marketing infrastructure to get their crops to market. USAID officials concur with this thesis and suggest that if the Bolivian farmer could get his alternative crop to market, he would do very well. However, the transporting and marketing challenges are beyond his capacity to organize (Clawson and Lee, 1993, pp. 34-35).

On the other hand, the drug lords provide that sorely needed infrastructure to the farmer. Roads are built adjacent to airstrips and vehicles are procured. Labor is supplied. All the farmer has to do is grow the crops with no overhead involved. The intimidation factor must also be recognized. It is not easy for the poor dirt farmer to "just say no" to a drug cartel and decide to plant a substitute crop. Such bold initiatives can lead not only to crop failure, but harassment and bodily injury.

The problem has more tentacles than just crop substitutes, infrastructure, or intimidation and the solution goes beyond just paying the farmer. The exploding population in the Andes is increasing the size of the available work force and coca growing is a lucrative source of employment for those who need work. From a demographics perspective, people will migrate to find this work.

In summary, the future of crop substitution is not promising. More than a decade of crop substitution programs in cocaine source countries have had little impact on the dynamics of Andean coca cultivation. There has been little actual crop substitution. The outlook for continued substitution programs appears bleak. The best arguments for retaining crop substitution programs are political rather than economic.

Again, although crop substitution may be thought of as a solution to the drug dilemma, not all Americans have supported this initiative. Quite the contrary, selected American institutions have doomed certain programs to failure. American farm lobbies blocked crop substitution programs that could have reduced Bolivia's coca exports. According to the GAO, "between 1988 and 1991, Washington lobbyists succeeded in blocking any aid for development of citrus and soy crops in the Andes on the grounds that they would increase competition with U.S. producers." (Clawson and Lee, 1993, pp. 1-3)

On balance, Clawson and Lee state that there has been a clear trend toward lower coca leaf prices over the last few years. In the late 1980's, a farmer could earn about $200 dollars for every 100 pounds of leaf (McCoy and Block, p. 4). Today that price is lower. It is estimated that the farmer needs to make $30 per 100 pound/leaf to break even. Thus, planting coca may not be as lucrative as it once was. There is an opportunity here for a carefully developed policy that enhances eradication and provides alternatives and infrastructure development to farmers. There have even been recommendations suggesting that the U.S. buy the entire coca crop in a nation. A Bolivian farmer can make $2600 per year per hectare growing coca, and according to calculations by Rensselear Lee it would cost the U.S. around $490 million to buy out the Bolivian crop (Smith, 1992, p. 118).

At first glance this may appear to be a ludicrous course of action. But historically, the U.S. has practiced such measures with wheat and other commodities in an effort to balance the market economy. Suppose they were to take half ($6.5 billion) of the annual drug budget and apply it toward buying out the coca crops in Latin America. The results could far exceed those eradication and interdiction tactics now employed. Intensive demand reduction programs, coupled with a quick drop in cocaine supply on the streets, could produce significant results.

## The Political Costs

The entire eradication and crop substitution strategy has far reaching political overtones, with North and South Americans blaming each other for the drug dilemma. Since the middle of the nineteenth century, the U.S. considered the Caribbean an "American Lake" and the nations of Latin America have been subjected to various forms of "made in America" solutions to domestic and regional problems. In recent discussions a former U.S. ambassador posted to a cocaine producing nation and a retired senior military Unified Commander have both strongly stated that U.S. policy with regard to counternarcotics must be carefully structured and executed so as to not only facilitate U.S. regional goals, but allow the nations their individual autonomy. More bluntly stated, America should stop mirror imaging and pushing U.S. policy down their throats. A 1992 *Newsweek* report quoted a senior Bolivian official as saying that "relations between the United States and Bolivia were narcoticized." (ONDCP Discussions, February 1994). On occasion, this type of "bull in the china shop" foreign policy alienates more than it helps to bring nations together in common objectives.

The Andean strategy for combatting illegal drugs, for example was born out of the Cartegena Summit. This strategy had four major objectives: strengthen the political will and internal capabilities of Bolivia, Peru, and Colombia; enhance the effectiveness of their military and law enforcement organizations in order to counter the cocaine industry; investigate and neutralize major trafficking organizations; and incorporate expanded economic assistance to help offset the costs of allocating money to fight drugs ((Lane and Larmer, 1992, pp. 18-23). These four objectives were based on three concepts: linkage, conditionality, and increased resources (Van Wert, 1992, p. 27). Moreover, President Bush linked controlling drugs to two other goals: promoting strong democracies and economies. The U.S. Congress allocated funds for these three Andean nations based on the condition that they effectively develop programs to thwart narcotics production and trafficking. The President would have to "certify" annually that progress was taking place in each of these nations. Based on this "carrot" certification, the nations collectively would receive $2.2 billion over a five year period (p. 27).

Over time, this strategy eroded in the eyes of the Andean national leaders and the follow-on San Antonio summit was a debacle. In a surprise to President Bush, Latin American leaders jointly decided to pull their militaries out of the drug fight. For the first time, Andean countries rebuffed America's strategies and goals, calling them unrealistic (pp. 26-27). More recently, President Gavaria of Colombia was reportedly indicted by his own nation's court system for unconstitutionally allowing U.S. military forces into his nation for suspected counternarcotics operations.

There are even critics who contend that Latin America is beyond help and that to disrupt the narcotics trade would cause a nation to collapse. As stated in "Dead End Drug Wars," "any U.S. strategy designed to significantly reduce the supply of cocaine at its source threatens the immediate economic viability of Andean countries and the political survival of Andean leaders." (Goldenberg, 1992, p. 401). This is the complete antithesis of the nation building policy.

## Drug Interdiction

America is an open nation and its borders are just too permeable. Given this reality, efforts to interdict drugs before they reach the streets are another instance where the country is doing poorly. To be sure, the U.S. interdicts drugs, often scoring big busts. Yet, as Skolnick suggests in his article, "Rethinking the Drug Problem," the interdiction efforts mainly catch the sloppy-poor trafficker, not the sophisticated dealers (Andreas et al, 1991, pp. 106-128). Frankly, "it would only take 13 trailer trucks to supply America's cocaine consumption for a year. Similarly, a 20 square mile field of opium poppies would meet the annual heroin demand." (Skolnick, 1992). While the data on how much cocaine is produced and subsequently how much flows into America is varied, roughly 1000 metric tons of cocaine are produced in Latin America. Of that figure, U.S. markets account for 300-420 metric tons, with the rest either going to other nations and being interdicted by law enforcement. However, according to the ONDCP, there is also evidence of significant warehousing of cocaine in the U.S. That should say to us that there is more supply than demand and that America does not interdict enough to affect demand on the street.

How much cocaine do U.S. authorities interdict? The estimates vary. High estimates suggest the country interdicts 30% of produced cocaine (ONDCP Discussions, 1994). Low estimates suggest that America only interdicts 3-12 % of inbound drugs (ONDCP Discussions, 1994). Estimates by senior officials working the U.S. southern border approximate a 10% interdiction rate which is probably a good mean figure (Goldstein, 1990, p. 22). Whatever estimates are used it is clear that trying to seal the border is mission impossible. The harder the country tries, the harder the drug lords work. Smuggling, therefore, has indeed evolved into a science.

Historically, there are parallels to the lift and shift operations described previously. As America puts more pressure on traffickers moving marijuana, they diversified their crop and moved to cocaine. So now, instead of moving large, hard to conceal and cheap drugs like marijuana, they are moving smaller, easily concealable and certainly more expensive drugs. Routes and patterns for trafficking are routinely upgraded to keep pace with law enforcement. For example, with the breakup of the French Connection due to international law enforcement efforts, the heroin trade shifted to other transshipment centers throughout the world. Nigeria is now a new center for the heroin trade (U.S. National Guard Discussions, 1994).

On balance, an increase in interdiction, albeit significant, would still do little to lower the street price of illegal drugs, especially since it is already low. If drug enforcement officials were able to double the interdiction rate to 60%, the effect on final retail price would be only 6% (Smith, 1992, p. 11). Other independent statistics support this argument. For example, Peter Reuter of the Rand Corporation points out that raising the cocaine interdiction rate from 20% to 50% would only marginally affect supply in the U.S., raising the street price only 4% per kilo (Staley, 1993, p. 200).

A subset of interdiction is the law enforcements' efforts to capture and prosecute key drug lords. The DEA has long contended that "drug kingpins" are the center of gravity, (Mabry, 1989, pp. 83-84) and there have been several successes in this area. Most recently was the surrender of the Cali Cartel leader, Julio Fabio Urdinola, which came a mere 100 days after the Medellin boss, Pablo Escobar, was killed by the Colombian authorities. It would appear that this is not a viable tactic. According to Guy Gugliotta, there is no evidence that the elimination of leaders brings a long term reduction in the cocaine trade. He cites examples such as the Gacha killing, the extradition of Carlos Lehder, and the imprisonment of Jose Ochoa (Mendel, 1992, p. 78). Yet the newest drug strategy still targets major cartels as a major strategy goal.

## Drug Substitution

Suppose America was able to eradicate and/or interdict all illegal drugs produced outside the borders. The problem is that as long as domestic demand is there, enterprising individuals will still meet most of this demand. Such is the case with the expanding synthetic drug market, as cited earlier. For example, methamphetamines such as "ice" and "crank" have become drugs of choice in many U.S. cities today, readily available and cheap to produce (Gugliotta, 1992, p. 125). As in every instance in studying the drug problem, there are qualifications to the expanding synthetic market. According to Peter Reuter, there is inadequate literature to substantiate the claim that synthetics will automatically replace the entire market demand for other illegal drugs due to a decreased supply of those drugs (Glastris, 1993, pp. 20-21). Evidence, albeit scarce, suggests that declines in imported drugs for whatever the reason are not fully compensated for by domestic production or diversion. Reuter claims "The existence of substitutes is not enough to justify nihilistic skepticism about the worth of international control programs." (Reuter, 1992, p. 173).

You be the judge. If you had a burning desire for a bourbon and water, but there was none available, what would you settle for: a beer or a soft drink? And even if all of the demand is not met by synthetic drugs, does it make sense to pour so much money into reducing the supply of foreign drugs if most of the demand would be met by synthetic drugs made at home?

## Money Laundering

The clandestine movement and reinvestment of narco-dollars has been a crucial ingredient to successful narcotics operations. On paper, the process is simple. It involves the disposal (placement) of cash from drug activity. The next step separates the illegal monies from their source through complex layers of financial transactions designed to hide the source and preempt an audit trail. Finally, the monies are retrieved through a legal transaction that is able to stand financial scrutiny, from all appearances being a normal business transaction (pp. 173-175). For example, the Cali cartel buys a bank in Colombia with a foreign office in Venezuela. A sizeable piece of real estate is bought in Venezuela by cartel members using illegal drug proceeds and the house is immediately sold for a loss. Moreover, the net result is clean money less the loss, which is an operating expense for doing business.

Many see defeating the money laundering schemes as the Achilles Heel of the illegal drug industry. "In matters of money, the cartels are particularly vulnerable because the same volume of business that insulates them from damage due to large cocaine seizures requires that they take considerable risk with their cash." (Zagaris, 1992, pp. 19-20). With the United States taking the lead, there have been quantum improvements in the efforts to control international money laundering. For instance, there have been numerous treaties such as the Vienna Drug Convention, meetings, declarations, and resolutions such as the G-7 Summit declaration and other Interpol initiatives (Gugliotta, 1992, p. 122). Successes have been noted with the Banco de Occidente and the BCCI, causing drug syndicates to spend additional time and money in re-circulating their laundering infrastructure (Zagaris, 1992, p. 41).

Unfortunately, just as we have discovered in our study of the drug syndicates, counter eradication and interdiction efforts, so too will the illegal money launderers become smarter in washing their money. Laundering will become more sophisticated with additional layering, new methods of legitimate transactions, the discovery of new jurisdictions to enter, and a diversification of investments (p. 41).

## The Interagency Mess

In examining several of the past White House assessments of the drug strategy, all touting progress in the war on drugs, one is overcome with the number of national programs: community partnerships, school and workplace programs, drug elimination grants, high risk use grants, demonstration grants, critical population grants, etc (p. 41). Each of these programs is well intended. But who is in charge? Where is the quality control? Certainly this is a legitimate concern when numerous agencies at the federal level alone are involved in countering the national drug problem. According to a 1991 study, there are 14 Federal agencies directly involved in drug law enforcement. This number does not represent those agencies indirectly involved, nor those agencies that manage the demand side of the national drug control strategy, nor the hundreds of state and local agencies working the issue. Some, not all, of the Federal drug law enforcement agencies (DLEA) are: the Drug Enforcement Administration; the Federal Bureau of Investigation; the Immigration and Naturalization Service; the Bureau of Alcohol, Tobacco, and Firearms; the Internal Revenue Service; the Coast Guard; the Federal Aviation Agency; the National Park Service and the Bureau of Land Management and Indian Affairs; the Department of Defense; and the State Department.

Even a novice to America's national political system would quickly conclude that cooperation and coordination between these agencies is not always congenial. Given the number of agencies involved in drug control efforts, it is not surprising to find strong differences of opinion and perspectives on how to solve the drug problem. Turf battles are thus routine in the competition for scarce resources. Overlapping jurisdictions further exacerbate this lack of harmony. Further, where is the synchronization between the Federal strategy and what the States and communities are doing? Frankly, no overall coordination among different levels of government was apparent during research for this study. On the contrary, coordination and lack of leadership seem to be the two major impediments to effective policy development and execution, both on the demand and supply sides of the house.

Over the last two decades there have been several initiatives to coordinate the overall national drug effort, such as Reagan's creation of the National Drug Enforcement Policy Board and Bush's creation of the Office of National Drug Control Policy (ONDCP). However, GAO and congressional reports have been consistently critical of leadership, coordination, and oversights within the drug control policy infrastructure, pointing out "continued inabilities to resolve long standing turf battles and delays in the implementation of mandated studies and programs." (White House, 1992). A tangential issue is the clash of interests and policy priorities. For example, the President of the United States under the provision of an aforementioned 1986 drug law can "de-certify" a nation for financial aid and assistance if it fails to cooperate fully with U.S. efforts in the region to curb drug production and trafficking. In 1988, President Reagan failed to de-certify Turkey, a major heroin trafficking nation. De-certification was requested by the DEA but disapproved by the State Department (Baglley, 1989, p. 48). Raphael Perl also identifies coordination weaknesses and calls for better leadership and management of the overall national drug program. He sees some optimism in the formation of the ONDCP and the attempts by its leadership to pull together the myriad of agencies and programs (p. 49).

Looking back on State and community coordination issues, there are strong arguments presented that clearly tie the effectiveness of any demand control program to the States and local communities. If America is ineffectively coordinated at the national level then a logical extrapolation would indicate that it is probably similarly ineffective at the local and State level. This complicates an already complex and imperfect system for the allocation and distribution of Federal dollars to State and local demand oriented programs.

The bottom line with these coordination and leadership challenges is that there are just too few dollars (in proportion to the rest of the budget) being spread over so many programs that no specific program has the real financial clout to be effective. Every one has a piece of the pie, but not enough to keep from starving, or in this case not enough dollars for any one program to be totally effective.

Mathea Falco's arguments fuel these concerns. Albeit that many of the demand programs have been tested and are working, she vigorously attacks past and current policies as being too thin. In her view, treatment programs are deficient in both quantity and quality. Prevention and education programs are too shallow and fail to inundate society at every level. Our community action programs are few and far between, although many of them have been very successful. Law enforcement focus is still lopsided: America's jails do not offer enough or effective treatment programs and drug use is still being assessed from the moralistic model vice the behavioral model. America's programs in research and development are lagging (Perl, 1992, p. 74).

Expanding on the law enforcement issue it is true that drug addicts and users are criminals. However, the law enforcement goal here must be weighted towards prevention and treatment. If America puts more police on the streets of our neighborhoods, it can become more preemptive than reactive. Don't give the opportunity for a crack house to develop, rather than trying to take it down later. Treatment programs, in consonance with, or as alternatives to incarceration, offer the best chance for success. The country must be tough, but merciful. For example, treatment, if refused, should be forced. Correctional treatment facilities should be constructed to allow the courts a place to send abusers and drug related criminals. This is being effectively done in Miami where drug courts funnel low level offenders into treatment vice jail. On the other hand, law enforcement should offer no quarter to the illegal producers and major traffickers. A distinction should also be made between the "hooked" and the profiteers.

Turning to research and development, one might ask why is it that in this age of miracle drugs and cures one should question why a preventative, or even a cure, for drug addiction has not been found. The answer may lie in the minuscule funding levels and the low priority given to research and development. What is interesting is that the bulk of research dollars are allocated toward supply oriented initiatives, such as advanced herbicides to destroy the coca crop. Here is an opportunity for intensive Federal management and reprioritization. The best and brightest of the nation's scientists should be put to task on this problem.

Wouldn't pure logic argue that a strategy weighted to reduce domestic drug use, and therein demand, would be easier to accomplish within the confines of America's own borders? The strategy would be insulated from geopolitical concerns and often awkward requirements for tactful international coordination. Indeed, the success stories with community action programs are striking. Look at community action in Tampa, Florida. A concerned minister coopted the city authorities and collectively reduced the street drug markets from 154 to 4 (Zuckerman, 1993, p. 74). Unequivocally, it was hard. It took money, but it worked. Does it not make sense to work the problem at its lowest level? Community programs are successful because drug abuse is in their backyard and it is not an impersonal concept. Historically, there has been a healthy desire to solve the problem at this level. But we have failed to understand this basic fact and fund it accordingly.

Top down leadership will not work in solving the drug problem in America's communities. It has been a long time, if ever, since the national leadership has been down in the "trenches" and they simply do not understand the problem like someone who lives with it daily. It is the cop on the beat, the clergy, the concerned citizen who must take the lead in this solution. "Weed and seed" programs, in which crime is targeted and then the community is "seeded" with prevention, education, and human resource services, require horizontal leadership within the community. Give the community grass-roots leaders federal resources and let them solve a problem all too close and known to them.

In fairness, the United States has never given demand oriented programs a fair shot at being successful. Before the hammer of criticism is lowered, it is appropriate to structure a viable demand strategy, fund it accordingly, and give it to the lowest level to execute. Over time, Americans will be surprised at how well it worked.

## References

Andreas, P. et al., (1991), "Dead End Drug Wars," *Foreign Policy*. Winter.

Bagley, B., (1989), "The New Hundred Years War,"*The Latin American Narcotics Trade and U.S. National Security*.

Carlucci, F., (1988), Role of the DOD in Drug Interdiction. A Joint Hearing before the House and Senate Committees on Armed Services, June 15.

Clawson, P. and Lee, R. (1993), "Crop Substitution in the Andes," *ONDCP Paper*, December.

Clawson, P. and Lee., R. (1992), "The Negative Economic, Political and Social Effects of Cocaine in Latin America," *ONDCP Study*.

Conner, R. and Burns, P. , (1992), "The Winnable War: How Communities are

Eradicating Local Drug Markets," *Brookings Review*, (Summer).

Cooper, M., (1993), "War on Drugs," *CQ Researcher*, March 19.

Dickert, J., (1992), "The Pentagon and the War on Drugs," *Case Study Written for the Kennedy School of Government*, Harvard University.

Dilulio, J., (1993), "The Next War on Drugs," *Brookings Review*. Summer.

Flynn, S. and Grant, G., (1993), "The Transnational Drug Challenge and the New World Order," The Center for Strategic and International Studies, Washington D.C.

Flynn, S., (1993), "Worldwide Drug Scourge: The Expanding Trade in Illicit Drugs," *Brookings Review*, Vol. 1, Winter.

Gene, J., (1992), "Losing Battles in the War on Drugs," *World Press Review*, June.

Glastris, P. , (1993), "The New Drug in Town," *U.S. News and World Report*. April 26.

Goldenberg, S., (1992), "War No More," *Nation*. March 30.

Goldstein, M., (1990), "Drug Wars, Turf Wars," *Government Executive*, 11 (January).

Gugliotta, G., (1992), "The Colombian Cartels and How to Stop Them," *Drug Policy in the Americas*, by Peter Smith.

Justice, U.S. Dept., (1992), "A National Report: Drugs, Crime, and the Justice System," *Bureau of Justice Statistics*, December.

Lane, C. and Larmer, B., (1992), *Newsweek*, January 6.

Lee, R., (1989), "The White Labyrinth, Cocaine and Political Power," New Brunswick: Transaction Publisher.

Levitsky, M., (1993), "Review of U.S. Efforts to Combat the International Narcotics Trade," *U.S. Department of State Dispatch*, Vol. IV, May 24.

Lykke, A., (1989), *Military Strategy: Theory and Application*. Carlisle Barracks, Pa.: U.S. Army War College, June 6.

Mabry, D., (1989), *The Latin American Narcotics Trade and U.S. National Security*.

Marcella, G., (1994), Notes during a lecture on Latin America presented at the U.S. Army War College

McCoy A. and Block, A., (1992), "U.S. Narcotics Policy: An Anatomy of Failure," *War on Drugs*. Boulder: Westview Press.

McDonald, S. and Zagaris, B., (1992), *International Handbook on Drug Control*, Westport: Greenwood Press.

Mendel W., (1992), "Elusive Victory," *Military Review*, December.

Moore, J., (1993), "Where did the Drug Crisis Go?," *National Journal*, February 20.

*Newsweek*, (1990), "A Mission to Nowhere," February 19.

*ONDCP Discussions*, (1994), February.

Perl, R., (1992), "The United States," *International Handbook on Drug Control*.

Reuter, P., (1992), "After the Borders are Sealed: Can Domestic Sources Substitute for Imported Drugs?," *Drug Policy in the Americas*.

46

Rosenberger, L., (1992), *Understanding Drug Abuse in American Society*. Carlisle Barracks, Pa: U.S. Army War College, Department of National Security and Strategy, August 1.

Skolnick, J., (1992), "Rethinking the Drug Problem", (Article from "Political Pharmacology: Thinking about Drugs) *Daedalus 121* (Summer)

Smith, P. , (1992), "The Political Economy of Drugs: Conceptual Issues and Policy Options," *Drug Policy in the Americas*. Westview Press.

Staley, S., (1993), "Drug Policy and the Decline of American Cities," *Transaction*.

Trumble, J., (1991),*USSOCOM Support for Counternarcotics.*U.S. Army War College, Pa: Research Paper.

U.S. National Guard Discussions, (1994).

Van Wert, J., (1992), "International Narcotics War: Bush's Other War — Are We Winning or Losing?," *War on Drugs: Studies in the Failure of U.S. Narcotics Policy*, edited by Alfred McCoy and Alan Block. Westview Press.

White House, (1992), U.S. National Drug Control Strategy.

Zagaris, B., (1992), "Money Laundering: An International Control Problem," International Handbook on Drug Control.

Zeese, K., (1991), "Drug War Forever," *Searching for Alternatives*. Melvyn Krauss and Ed Lazear, eds., Stanford: Hoover University Press.

Zimring, F. and Hawkins, G., (1992), *The Search for Rational Drug Control*.

Zukerman, M., (1993), "Fighting the Right Drug War," *U.S. News and World Report*. April 26.

# 5  Clinton's Strategy

The election of Bill Clinton to the Presidency in November 1992 raised hopes of a fundamental change in U.S. drug policy. After all, President Clinton was elected on a domestic oriented platform that promised to shift America's focus inward. At last, Washington would have an opportunity to address those domestic problems that had been neglected by his predecessors during the days when national security was defined primarily in a foreign policy context. Perhaps President Clinton and a Democratic Congress would also use this opportunity to focus national drug control policy on reducing the demand for drugs at home.

## Policy Drift and Rumors

During the first year of his Presidency, President Clinton seemed totally preoccupied with putting a budget together. But what about the drug control part of the budget? How should the money be spent in controlling drugs? In fact, was there still a drug war out there somewhere? Hard to tell. For that matter, was there even a drug problem anymore?

All was too quiet on the drug front. The American public just seemed to drift away from the drug issue. And so too did their President. The drug war "hype" was also noticeably absent from the White House. If interested parties were afraid that Bill Clinton would put drug policy on the back burner, they soon learned that Bill Clinton wanted it off the stove entirely. In fact, the signals from the Oval Office were quite clear. During the so called "Saturday night massacre," President Clinton actually cut the number of personnel in the Office of National Drug Control Policy (ONDCP) from 146 to 25.

The contrast with the Bush years was especially striking. Only a couple of months before Clinton's arrival, the Bush "War on Drugs" was raging. Now a *New York Times* article was blasting President Clinton's slowness in forming a national drug policy and allowing key positions to remain open. It also criticized the

Clintonites for putting the drug budget on automatic pilot, which meant following the glide path of the previous Republican administrations. Since drug policy was considered a low priority to the Clintonites that first year, no attempt was made to raise supplemental funds for drastically underfunded demand side programs (*New York Times*, 1993, editorial, April 22, p. 24).

Other observers were more pointed in their policy advocacy advice for President Clinton. For instance, the *American Journal of Public Health* called for beefed up prevention measures for the youth of America. Still others recommended drug courts and treatment in lieu of jail (Jay, D. 1993, pp. 793-795; Zuckerman, M. 1993, p. 74).

In the absence of policy clarity, leaks and rumors began to percolate about what would actually emerge in the final draft of a Clinton national drug control strategy. Several early press reports stated that the President was on the verge of a major shift in drug control strategy. He purportedly would move the United States from a supply side emphasis to a demand side focus (*U.S. News and World Report*, 1993, Sept. 27, p. 83).

Some reports were more specific and suggested the new policy would cut military and economic assistance to Latin American governments (Douglas, J. 1993, p. 8. Still other press reports argued that the Bush administration's dismantling of the drug labs had been effective, but that the interdiction program was a dismal failure (NYT, 1993, Sept. 16, p. 16). This report was consistent with a later story that stated that the interdiction budget would be cut by 11% and the difference would be redirected towards health measures (Treaster, J. 1993, p. a6).

In the midst of all of this political infighting, policy formulation and media play, the President announced the appointment of former New York Police Commissioner Lee Brown as Drug Czar. Before coming to Washington Lee Brown had sharply criticized the Bush administration's drug strategy saying, "I look at the message coming out of Washington that we are winning the drug war and I don't know what city they are talking about." (Buckley, W. 1993, p. 71).

With tough words like this, the public and private sectors could logically expect a major shift in policy from their new Drug Czar. And Lee Brown was not the only major player in the administration who was critical of previous policies and strategies. The new Attorney General, Janet Reno, also questioned some aspects of the drug policy, especially efforts to block smuggling of drugs into the United States. She stated it was not cost effective and vowed to take steps to make treatment more available to drug users (Labaton, S. 1993, May 8, p. 9).

## Supply Reduction Versus Demand Reduction

While it took awhile for Bill Clinton to get out of the starting blocks on drug policy, a close examination of the 1994 Strategy reveals significant departures from the earlier Republican strategies. It was also a radical departure from what even the Democratically controlled Congress was prepared for in the early 1990s. It was filled with innovative new ideas. Unfortunately, President Clinton never put enough political capital and enthusiasm into the document to sell it to his own Democratic leadership on Capital Hill.

The first major issue the Clinton administration had to address in its policy formulation for the 1994 strategy was how much money to spend on supply side reduction programs versus demand side reduction programs. The mandate for this decision comes from the Anti-Drug Abuse Act of 1988. This act requires the Federal Government to produce a comprehensive National Drug Control Strategy, detailing the resources committed to implement it. It calls for a balanced, comprehensive strategy and mandates that Federal drug strategies be classified as supply reduction or demand reduction programs.

Initially at least, the Clinton White House tried to avoid making the politically explosive choice between demand and supply side resources. It rejected the premise that supply reduction programs and demand reduction programs had to compete against each other. The Clintonites tried to make the theoretical case that it was time for the demand and supply side fiefdoms to "bury the hatchet" and work together to develop an integrated strategy. And so they argued that demand reduction programs (including drug treatment, prevention, and education) cannot succeed if drugs are readily available and that drug enforcement programs cannot ultimately succeed if the Nation's appetite for illegal drugs is not curbed.

In this sense, the Clintonites made a theoretically logical case that the demand side reduction and supply side reduction programs were synergistic. They rejected what they called the "false choice" between demand reduction and law enforcement efforts. They felt the United States needed more money spent in both areas. And so in the 1994 Strategy document, its FY 1995 wish list for drug control spending, called for $1 billion in additional money for both supply reduction and demand reduction programs. For example, while 1994 Strategy called for the largest ever increase in funds dedicated for the treatment of hardcore users and redoubled prevention efforts aimed at youth, it also requested substantial increases to State and local enforcement, primarily to put more police on America's streets.

While the Clinton administration tried to win over the supply side fiefdom with additional resources, it was clear that the Clinton White House wanted to shift the emphasis to demand side reduction. If one looks at the small print, the bulk of the requested increase in total drug control resources was for demand reduction programs. The Clintonites wanted demand reduction programs to increase by more than 18 percent as compared with supply reduction programs which they wanted increased by only 3 percent.

To be sure, the supply side camp still was to receive a much larger share of the overall drug control budget than the demand side camp. Of the total $13.2 billion request for drug control programs, $7.8 billion was to go for supply reduction programs and while only $5.4 billion was slated for demand reduction programs. In other words, the FY 1995 budget request provided 59 percent of total budgeted resources for supply reduction and 41 percent for demand reduction programs. Thus, the supply side fiefdom was still larger than the demand side camp, but it was beginning to shrink as a share of the overall pie. The percentage of resources for supply reduction was slated to fall below 60 percent for the first time in recent memory.

This proposed new supply/demand mix reflected a dramatic shift in program emphasis in favor of treatment and prevention programs. It also demonstrated the Clinton Administration's initial commitment to closing the gap between funding for supply reduction and demand reduction programs. At the same time, this proposed shift was perceived as an direct threat to the turf of the supply side fiefdom. This supply side fiefdom includes two politically powerful groups. The first group consists of senior military officers who value the additional training and hardware dollars they receive for what many privately concede is strategically futile. The second group are the supply side bureaucrats who command "LMDs" (Long Mohogany Desks) in Washington's interagency jungle.


**Congress Supports Supply Siders**

Regardless of one's views on the demand/supply mix, President Clinton's intent was clearly designed to beef up the demand reduction side of the drug control strategy while at the same time creating a more innovative supply reduction strategy. But realistic goals and creative concepts are not enough. To turn a dream into a strategy takes resources. In other words, we need to judge the potential success or failure of President Clinton drug control strategy on the of basis of its stated ends, ways and means (Lykke, 1993).

Generally speaking, the money President Clinton requested for FY 1995 and the total dollars Congress appropriated (approximately the same) would have improved the situation on the demand front. Unfortunately, Congress had different ideas. The programs Congress chose to appropriate money for differed significantly from President Clinton's original FY 1995 request. In essence, the actual FY 1995 drug control budget reflects Congressional success in killing President Clinton's original attempt to shift resources to demand reduction.

The money Congress authorized to be spent in FY 1995 put about the same emphasis on supply reduction as its predecessor in FY 1994. Supply side reduction programs (as a percentage of the total drug budget) deceased only from FY 1994 63.7 % in FY 1994 to an estimated 62.8 % in FY 1995. In short, Congress underfunded many of the key demand side budget initiatives sought by President Clinton.

What was particularly frustrating to the Clintonites was their inability to persuade a Democratically controlled Congress to move away from a lopsided supply side strategy. On drug policy, the Democratically controlled Congress in the early 1990s and the Republican controlled Congress in the mid 1990s had much

51

in common. Both wanted the large supply reduction programs to remain intact and neither wanted to increase spending on demand reduction programs. The main distinction between Republicans and Democrats on Capital Hill was in how much to cut Clinton's initial efforts to increase spending on prevention and treatment programs.

The additional law enforcement (supply side) funds for drug control provided by Congress for FY 1995 resulted from the passage of the 1994 Crime Control Act. The 1994 Crime Control Act continues to drive FY 1996 drug control spending and to keep the same emphasis on reducing the supply of drugs. While the Crime Control Act is a creative and welcome new approach to address the supply reduction side of the drug problem, it is no substitute for a beefed up demand side strategy. In other words, the Crime Control Act realistically comes at the expense of necessarily more robust demand reduction programs.

## A Fresh Look at Drug Control

But it was not just the overall thrust of the Clinton's new demand side strategy that gave Congress heartburn. Congress was troubled by a number of new initiatives that Clinton was pushing in his 1994 Strategy. But before we examine specific initiatives, we need to ask even more fundamental questions. For instance, what was the reasoning behind Clinton's original intent to shift resources to demand reduction? What were his overall drug control goals? How did President Clinton expect to reach these goals? And how could supply reduction programs complement demand reduction programs?

From 1988 to 1994, the U.S. Government spent more than $52 billion on drug related efforts. During this period, the Republican strategies had placed special emphasis on reducing of casual or intermittent drug use. Casual or intermittent drug users were people whose frequency of drug use did not result in problems or behaviors that required some type of treatment. That being the case, most members of Congress felt that there was not much reason to spend a lot of money on treatment.

While America achieved some successes in reducing the overall amount of casual or intermittent drug use during this period, illegal drugs continued to pose a significant threat to America. Most troubling to the incoming Clinton administration was the fact that hardcore drug use continued unabated. Similarly, drug related crime and violence did not drop significantly either. In this regard, Clinton's 1994 strategy correctly linked drug abuse and crime. The Clintonites argued that since drug using offenders are responsible for a disproportionate amount of crime, and because the frequency and severity of their criminal activity rises dramatically during periods of heavy or addicted use, treating hardcore addicts would logically help reduce drug-related crime (1994 Strategy)

While the overarching goal of Clinton's 1994 National Drug Control Strategy was the reduction of all kinds of drug use in America, the 1994 strategy expanded the focus away from just casual and intermittent drug use and placed it correctly on the most difficult and problematic drug-using population — hardcore drug users. In other words, first and foremost, the 1994 Strategy made the reduction of drug use by hardcore drug users its number one priority.

While this approach made good theoretical sense, it exposed Clinton politically. Congress tended to want a more punitive approach to hard core drug abusers as well as drug pushers. By arguing for more drug treatment money to help hard core drug abusers inside and outside the criminal justice system, it exposed the Clinton administration to the charge that it was squandering the money of good Americans to "coddle" the drug habits of self destructive, bad Americans.

This philosophical difference between the Clintonites and Congress became evident during the implementation of the Anti-Drug Abuse Act of 1988. In addition to the mandate calling for the President to classify drug control resources as demand reduction versus supply reduction, this act requires clear and measurable goals for drug control programs.

With an estimated 2.7 million hardcore users on the streets, and with Americans spending $49 billion annually on illegal drugs, the Clinton administration developed the following objectives. For hard core drug use, the objective was to reduce the number of hardcore users through drug treatment at an average annual rate of 5 percent. For casual or intermittent drug use, the objective was also to reduce the number of casual or intermittent drug users at an average annual rate of 5 percent.

### Reducing Hardcore Drug Use Through Treatment

The Clinton White House began with the premise that treatment could decisively reduce hard core drug use and its consequences to both users as well as society. It cites recent estimates that as many as 2.5 million users could benefit from drug treatment. Unfortunately, only about 1.4 million users were treated in 1993. The Clintonites argue that it was largely because of inadequate public funding that 1.1 million users did not have the opportunity to receive drug treatment. To reduce this shortfall, President Clinton wanted to expand treatment capacity and services and increase treatment so that those that need it can receive it. The President was seeking to target intensive services for hard core drug using populations and special populations, including adults and adolescents in custody or under supervision of the criminal justice system. He also wanted to target pregnant women and women with dependent children. In order to reach this goal, Clinton wanted a sharp increase in spending for drug treatment. Consequently, President Clinton's FY 1995 funding request for drug treatment programs was $2.9 billion, an increase of $360 million (or 14.3 percent).

The Clinton White House came up with two new initiatives for drug treatment. First, a $355 million FY 1995 request to enhance drug treatment capacity nationwide, targeting treatment for chronic, hardcore drug users, who are the heaviest users and consume the bulk of the illegal drugs. The bulk of this money was to go to the Department of Health and Human Services (HHS) for its Substance Abuse Prevention and Treatment Block grant. Second, $200 million was requested to go for enhanced treatment capacity within the criminal justice system through drug courts, which provide treatment services to help individual users get off drugs rather than a more traditional punitive response.

This level of requested treatment funding would have provided treatment for up to an additional 74,000 hardcore drug users. In addition, the proposed crime bill would provide resources for treatment to as many as 65,000 additional hardcore users in prisons. With this in mind, the 1994 strategy proposed to increase the number of hardcore drug users getting treatment by almost 140,000 per year beginning in FY 1995. This number includes hardcore drug users both inside and outside the criminal justice system. The Clinton White House correctly points out that providing treatment is both a compassionate and a pragmatic course of action. According to the National Institute on Drug Abuse (NIDA), every dollar spent on drug treatment saves $4 — $7 in reduced costs to the public and $3 in increased productivity.

Unfortunately, congressional appropriations for these treatment initiatives were a far cry from President Clinton's FY 1995 requests. For instance, HHS only received $57.0 million for its Substance Abuse Prevention and Treatment Block grant. Similarly, the Department of Justice only received $29 million for Drug Courts. In short, Congress chose to drastically underfund the key drug treatment initiatives that would have made a significant difference in reducing hard core drug use in America in FY 1995.

In retrospect, President Clinton deserves high marks for at least trying to move in the right direction, even if his early efforts to persuade American people and Congress could have been more energetic. Clinton's strategy called for increasing the number of hard core drug users undergoing treatment by 140,000 annually. This was an exceptionally noble objective. But a penny wise, dollar foolish Congress killed these programs in their tracks. The Clintonites also wanted to enact the first ever guarantee of basic drug use treatment services as part of the President's Health Security Act. At a minimum, this would have provided basic substance abuse treatment benefits to the more than 58 million Americans without coverage. Unfortunately, this promising treatment initiative became a victim of the Republican success in killing President Clinton's overall health care plan.

The real costs of killing these programs will be much higher costs for the American people in the longer term. By turning its back on drug treatment programs, Congress has triggered a chain reaction of more drug use, more emergency room visits and more crime. The real costs to the American people will skyrocket and will appear in the demand for more jails and prisons, larger police departments, higher insurance rates, higher health care premiums, and fewer health benefits to pay for all of these second and third order costs.

## Adjusting the War on Drugs Overseas

Initially at least, the Clintonites also wanted to change the thrust of the international war on drugs. Many members of the incoming Clinton White House team were critical of the Bush Administration's decision to use the U.S. military in the futile task of trying to seal the U.S. border. Not only did many of the Clintonites view this military mission of trying to stop the flow of drugs across the U.S border an abysmal failure (no dramatic rise in the price of cocaine in America), but they also correctly perceived interdiction as a huge waste of money.

But selling a radical change to Congress and the supply side fiefdom would prove to be just as difficult as trying to beef up demand side programs. When the dust settled in the interagency arena, interdiction did not go away. Instead there were small adjustments in policy rather than radical changes. In November 1993, a watered down compromise known as Presidential Decision Directive (PDD) 14 emerged from a bloody interagency battle.

PDD-14 recognized that the availability of drugs in America had not been significantly reduced despite all of the money that had been spent on the supply side of this drug war. But if Americans had any inclination that dramatic change would mark the forthcoming Clinton strategy, PDD-14 dampened such expectations and reinforced DOD's continued role in counterdrug operations. PDD-14 did not get the U.S. military out of the strategically futile interdiction game. Instead, PDD-14 stressed more selective and flexible interdiction programs near the U.S. border, in the transit zone, and in the source countries (White House, 1993, Nov. 3, p. 1).

In addition, PDD-14 reportedly identified international criminal narcotics syndicates as a national security threat (p. 1). To counter this threat, PDD-14 directed federal agencies to change their modus operandi in three program areas. First, it directed the relevant agencies to use assistance for sustainable development to address the root causes of narcotics production and trafficking. Second, it called for strengthening of democratic institutions. Third, it called for cooperative programs with friendly governments to combat international narco-traffickers, money laundering, and the supply of chemical precursor agents" (White House, 1993, Nov. 3, p. 1).

Much of the thinking that went into PDD-14 reappeared in a more comprehensive way in Clinton's 1994 National Drug Control Strategy. It called for supporting supply reduction programs worldwide. In particular, the strategy called for supporting, implementing, and leading more successful enforcement efforts to increase the costs and risks to narcotics producers and traffickers in hopes of reducing the supply of illicit drugs to the United States. In order to improve the national response to organized international drug trafficking, the budget request emphasized programs that support a controlled shift of resources from the transit zones to source countries.

At the heart of the strategy is the conviction that the U.S. should cooperate with and support other nations that share the U.S. political will to defeat the international drug syndicates. The Clintonites wanted to enhance international programs to give producer countries the means to attack the problems of drug production and trafficking at the sources. In this regard, Clinton's 1995 budget requested an increase of $72 million for the Department of State and Agency for International Development to support source country efforts to reduce the availability of illicit drugs through a number of activities.

The Clintonites, for instance, wanted to intensify international efforts to arrest and imprison international drug kingpins and destroy their organizations. In addition, the strategy called for aggressively supporting crop control programs for poppy and coca in countries where there is a strong prospect for or record of success. They also wanted to strengthen host nation counternarcotics institutions (e.g. training of law enforcement personnel and judicial reform) so that they could conduct more effective drug control efforts on their own. Other activities fell in the categories of sustainable development, interdiction, eradication and demand reduction.

How promising were some of these international goals? Let's look at the goal of assisting other nations in developing and implementing comprehensive counternarcotics policies that strengthen democratic institutions and destroy narcotrafficking in both the source and the transit countries. This goal concentrates U.S. assistance on building effective judicial, law enforcement, and social infrastructures in key drug producing nations. This objective will probably be blended with continued U.S. encouraged eradication operations in those nations. Once again, this goal is a link to previous supply oriented strategies. It will compete with demand programs for scarce dollars. And if the past is an indicator, funds will be available at the expense of domestic programs.

On the other hand, Clinton's effort to strengthen international cooperation against narcotic production and trafficking and drug use is more promising. Drug abuse is a global problem and the solution must, therefore, be global in nature. Here, the U.S. promises to take the lead in enhancing multilateral organizations such as the United Nations, the World Bank, etc. Also, DOD can expect to continue its role in training foreign police forces and in strengthening host nation counternarcotics institutions. Potentially, this approach could conceivably complement a demand oriented national drug strategy by allocating effort to more cost effective international initiatives, rather than continued interdiction and eradication operations.

## Domestic Law Enforcement

One area that continues to get ample funding from Congress is traditional domestic law enforcement. President Clinton's 1994 National Drug Control Strategy discusses a number of domestic law enforcement goals. These goals include reducing all domestic drug production and availability, improving the efficiency of federal law enforcement capabilities and reducing domestic drug related crime and violence. These are all worthwhile objectives. But how promising are these domestic supply reduction goals given the nature and extent of the demand for drugs in America?

The first goal is exceedingly ambitious. President Clinton seeks to reduce all domestic drug production and availability and to continue to target for investigation and prosecution those who illegally import, manufacture, and distribute dangerous drugs and who illegally divert pharmaceuticals and listed chemicals. In essence, this is the same old supply side domestic strategy, the focus of which is to aggressively target major narcotics trafficking organizations. Interdiction operations are implied and certainly DOD will have a continued or even expanded role in trying to translate this elusive goal into action.

The second goal is also ambitious. President Clinton seeks to improve law enforcement capabilities by beefing up intelligence and interdiction activities. The assumption here is that pouring more money into high technology will somehow make a difference in the amount of drugs pouring into the United States. This goal also complements the previous one by directing increased interagency coordination. Without a doubt, any effort to streamline the national drug command, control and coordination process is a good idea.

## Diminishing Resources

Euphoria quickly dissipated when the entire scope of the strategy was placed in the context of diminishing resources. Despite all of these impressive goals, the reality of the new strategy is that resources fall way too short. Although the FY 95 budget called for $13.2 billion, this is a minuscule amount when allocated to buy a strategy with fourteen extremely ambitious goals. Of all the aforementioned goals, five appear to be solidly based in past strategies, with 59% of allocated funds supporting them. Only 41% ($5.4 billion) goes toward the other nine demand/domestic oriented goals.

Where is the money going to come from? The struggling entitlement system? Unfortunately, the new drug strategy appears to be a panacea for every player. One could argue that the strategy is more politically (constituent) oriented than designed to really solve the problem.

Although the strategy goes into some detail on "how to" accomplish all of the drug control goals, there is a gross lack of specifity that leads one to question whether it is more a paper plan instead of a substantive solution.

Things are only getting worse in late 1995. The November 1995 U.S. government shutdown and the partial U.S. government shutdown in December 1995 are merely the most recent and dramatic examples of the pressure being placed on all U.S. government programs in these fiscally troubled times. Drug abuse programs are certainly no exception.

In his 1995 Strategy document, President Clinton is requesting about $14.6 billion for drug control programs in FY 1996. As of late January 1996, we still don't have a FY 1996 drug control budget despite the fact that a quarter of the FY 1996 fiscal year has come and gone. While much is still up in the air, a few things are reasonably clear in regards to the drug policy budget. The Republican controlled Congress is determined to cut about $1 billion out of President Clinton proposed budget. About 70% of these cuts will come from two important demand reduction programs. In addition, the percentage of the overall drug control budget going to demand reduction programs would decrease from President Clinton's FY 1996 request of 36% to only about 34% if the proposed Congressional cuts remain intact.

The first program, Safe and Drug Free Schools and Communities (SDFSC), is designed to prevent children and adolescents from getting hooked on drugs. The House wants to cut about 60 % of the funds for this worthwhile program. If successful, this House action would affect 97 % of the Nation's public schools at a time when drug use by children and adolescents is going up across the country. The Senate would only cut 20 % of SDFSC funds and transfer these to another part of the drug control budget. Exactly what will emerge from a House/Senate conference on this program is not clear at this point. But sharp cuts are almost certain (ONDCP Discussions, December 1995)

The second program on the cutting block, Substance Abuse and Mental Health Services Administration (SAMHSA), is divided about equally between the treatment as well as the prevention of drug abuse. The House and the Senate want to cut about 30 % of President Clinton's SAMHSA request for FY 1996. The impact of these cuts would be to deny treatment to about 40,000 hard core drug addicts.

On the supply side, President Clinton wanted a controlled shift of emphasis from the futile task disrupting the flow of cocaine in the transit zones to a more balanced, long term and integrated approach that helps countries like Colombia attack the drug producers at the source. The congressional appropriation committees responsible for transit spending were willing to make some spending reductions but were unwilling to shift resources to the committees responsible for spending money in source countries. As a result, Congress is only willing to fund about $115 million of President Clinton's $213 FY 1996 request for the State Department's Bureau of International Narcotics and Law Enforcement Affairs program for source countries. (ONDCP Discussions, December 1995)

President Clinton is likely to veto some of these congressional cuts. The government may shut down once more. But after all is said and done, President Clinton's drug control strategy will almost certainly not get the resources needed to successfully reach many of his goals. This is particularly true in the area of demand reduction. What is to be done now?

## Time for a New Strategy

Let's begin by reassessing Clinton's overall drug control strategy. In doing so, it's clear that most of it is driven from Washington. While the strategy has a number of worthwhile community action programs (which we will discuss later), these initiatives tend to be relatively small parts or tactics in the overall top down, lop-sided supply reduction strategy.

No government (Federal, State or local) can solve the problem by itself. But the conservative efforts in 1995 to shut down worthwhile federal drug policy programs simply runs away from the problem. Something must take their place or else the drug abuse problem will worsen. We need to build a new national political consensus that promotes stronger community based institutions to tackle drug problems. They may be what President Bush liked to call "points of light." But George Bush also created a myth: that private groups and individual charity could replace government. They cannot.

But creative and energetic nonprofit organizations can and do form cost effective partnerships with government to provide better services together than either could do independently. In this sense, these points of light burn more brightly with government support than on their own, even if this funding is likely to be much smaller in the future. Our challenge is to creatively connect these community organizations to diminishing U.S. government resources without strangling them with regulation and red tape (Garr, p. viii).

Robin Garr provides a set of principles to guide a bottoms up strategy. He argues that government should support community organizations that:

- are guided by clear objectives
- foster self-reliance by building people's strengths
- use a holistic approach, bringing the full range of tools to bear on each individual's problems
- deal with individuals, one-on-one
- focus on prevention
- demonstrate strong leadership

In these fiscally troubled times, we need to make a virtue out of a necessity by turning the fiscal roadblocks into opportunity for action. We need to adjust top down programs from Washington that depend on the old federal programs, which in turn are the inventions of office bound bureaucrats or policy gurus. The new approach reflects the common sense ideas of everyday Americans who see a problem and do what they can to fix it (Garr, p. vii)

One such common sense organization is Cafe 458 in Atlanta, Georgia. Cafe 458 is a non-profit restaurant designed and built by volunteers. It serves a select group of diners who get referred from social service agencies. They earn the right to eat at the cafe by agreeing to take part in programs designed to ease them back into the community. Food is the hook that brings people together for conversation. It's the way to develop relationships that allow people to talk about their problems.

Betty Voight serves as a Recovery counselor in the residential program for treating long-term drug and alcohol abuse at Cafe 458. She says that "what we're really about is building relationships with people . . . making them feel welcome. We play music. We put flowers on the tables. We listen. People tell us their stories and we tell ours. It opens people to the process of transformation" (Garr, p. 13)

Betty Voight agrees with the Clintonites on the importance of linking drug abuse programs to other social programs. She persuasively argues that "the more we become involved in drug and alcohol abuse, the more we learn how entrenched homelessness and chemical abuse and poverty and loss of self esteem all mesh together" (Garr, p. 13). And so we cannot just focus on drug abuse, nor can we simply provide a band-aid or quick fix that addresses the symptoms of the drug abuse problem. Grass-roots organizations that successfully turn people's lives around take the time to identify every problem that stands between an individual and recovery. In short, we must use a holistic approach to reduce drug abuse.

In addition, we can not reduce drug abuse treatment to an assembly line. We must deal with individuals one on one. The Recovery Program in Atlanta's Cafe 458 is a good example of this principle. The counsellors at Cafe 458 only work with a dozen homeless drug addicts at a time. They give the drug addicts food, conversation, emotional support and love. While they would love to treat thousands of hard core addicts, the counsellors focus more profitably on only a handful of individuals at a time.

Admittedly, the Recovery program at Cafe 458 follows a slow, daily, long term, painstaking path. But rushing people or putting then into herds solves nothing. We cannot take people with deep-seated problems and mass-produce them overnight into drug free, mentally healthy people. In contrast to the large government run programs, the recovery programs that work provide warmth and humanity. A personal touch is what promotes the all important self-esteem that in turn paves the way to reach the ultimate goals of self-reliance and individual responsibility (Garr, p. 234).

Developing self-esteem and self-reliance are the critical concepts behind Recovery. About ten men live in a safe, clean home provided by a church, where they receive personal counselling and work in small in-house businesses. The program lets recovering addicts gradually ease back into the routine of taking personal responsibility for their life. Its success is dramatically different from the norm in the drug treatment business. While as many as 90 percent of the graduates of drug and alcohol programs nationally relapse after six months, nine out of ten Recovery graduates stay clean (Garr, p. 13).

## Clinton's Community Action Programs

President Clinton is philosophically comfortable with these kinds of grass-roots community actions and would seem open to the idea of expanding these programs. Not only are the Clinton administration community action programs innovative and generally successful, they hold great promise in a fiscally constrained period. In this sense, they could be politically attractive to conservatives on Capital Hill if President Clinton were to invest real political capital in expanding them and selling them to the American people.

President Clinton correctly says that US government can not solve this hard core drug use problem by itself. As part of their 1993 strategy, the Clinton administration argues that success in controlling the drug problem also depends on help from local governments at home as well as foreign governments overseas. The Clintonites argue that local communities need to be empowered with an integrated plan of education, prevention, treatment and law enforcement.

While community action in general makes sense, there is a political down side for President Clinton. Frankly, it is a hard sell. The pitch exposes President Clinton politically to all of those Americans who expect Washington to come up with a silver bullet solution to the "war on drugs." Here is a U.S. President shifting much of the intellectual and blue collar work back onto the shoulders of the stressed out voter. After being conditioned to think the U.S. military could help win the war on drugs, the American people are now being told to become foot-soldiers in what seems like another unwinnable war. Getting Americans to roll up their sleeves and do what government used to do is necessary in a fiscally troubled era. But it's a hard sell politically (See Haifetz, R. 1995).

Nonetheless, in his 1994 National Drug Control Strategy, President Clinton argues that the success of the strategy ultimately rests on the ability of participants to work at the grass-roots level in neighborhoods and communities throughout the Nation in order to effectively achieve their goals and objectives. In other words, the strategy is truly national in scope and its success is not just a Federal responsibility.

In his 1994 strategy President Clinton correctly argues that the most effective strategies for preventing drug use and keeping drugs out of neighborhoods and schools are those that mobilize all elements of a community coalitions such as those sponsored by the Department of Health and Human Services. The best of these coalitions establish and sustain a strong partnership among businesses, schools, religious groups, social services organizations, law enforcement, the media, and community residents to help rid the neighborhood of drugs and drug-related violence. In this way, they keep the community safe and free from the fear that pervades communities plagued by drug problems.

In addition, individuals, families, neighbors, churches and synagogues, and civic and fraternal organizations must work together to forge efforts to address the underlying causes of social disintegration within their communities in order to prevent drug use. In this sense, we cannot address the drug problem in a vacuum. Often it is inextricably linked with urban decay, poverty, crime, and education.

Those of us who are concerned about drug abuse must link up with other grassroots movements that are reinvesting in America by feeding the hungry, housing the homeless and putting America back to work. In particular, there is a need for treatment providers to be better linked to programs that offer related vocational and social services for hardcore drug users. The grass-roots organizations that are most successful are those which network with other local organizations fighting similar battles. (Garr, 1995, p. ix).

The good news is that Clinton's 1994 Strategy includes strong linkages between other, non-drug related social programs. The bad news is that many domestic policy programs are top down programs which conservatives in Congress are watering down in the name of a balanced budget. The same fate is plaguing Clinton's drug policy. If the individual components that support an effective domestic oriented drug control strategy are weak (ie, crime reduction, education, urban renewal, etc) the overall drug strategy will never reach fruition. We need a bottom up strategy across the board if drug policy is to be truly successful.

Health care is a good case in point. The 1994 Drug Control Strategy tried to weave in Clinton's national health care plan, which went nowhere with Congress. Was Clinton building a major component of its new drug strategy (treatment and prevention) on sand? Did it make sense to drop four million people who meet the clinical criteria for drug dependency on a fledgling health care program? Did the two program directors, Lee Brown and Hillary Clinton, even talk with each other about four million additional clients? And what about the aforementioned 1996 goal that would offer drug abuse treatment for some 58 million uninsured Americans?.

Similarly, just as all of the domestic programs must smoothly mesh at the local level, there must also be a commitment by all levels of government to succeed at the community level. Clinton's 1994 National Drug Control Strategy recognizes the importance of Federal, State and local government program linkages and the need for grassroots level efforts rather than top-down Federal-to-local programs to deal with the drug problems. To that end, there is a strong need for better cross-agency coordination with regard to drug programs as well as more flexibility for communities to allocate resources in areas that will best meet their particular circumstances. This new Strategy calls for all levels of government to participate vigorously with state and local governments, private organizations and foundations, interest groups, religious organizations, and private citizens if it is to be successful.

This new grass-roots, neighborhood strategy also requires a shift to a new model of public funding for private, community based organizations. Government provides financing and appropriate oversight to the grassroots organizations, which in turn provide the competent, caring service at the local level (Garr, p. 7). While the initiative must come from community leaders, the role of the Federal government should not be minimized. In addition to leveraging financial and other resource support, the Federal Government can create an atmosphere where successful community-based antidrug efforts are welcomed, fostered, and developed. In this way, the role of government at all levels in the future may be one of empowering the entrepreneurial and administrative skills of individuals to rebuild their own communities.

A good example of what can be done in this regard is President Clinton's commitment to community efforts to revitalize our neighborhoods and provide an opportunity to help communities help themselves. The President realizes that there is a need to empower communities with an integrated plan of education, prevention, treatment and law enforcement. This plan calls for the expansion of the number of cooperative efforts, such as community coalitions, by targeting the most disadvantaged urban and rural areas — communities often hit hardest by drug abuse and drug-related crime and violence.

With a bottom up approach in mind, President Clinton established Community Empowerment Zones and Enterprise Communities. These programs designate up to 104 areas that meet certain poverty and distress criteria and prepare strategic plans for revitalization. All 9 Empowerment Zones and all 95 Enterprise Communities must address drug use, trafficking, and prevention in their community-based empowerment plans.

To make sure there was sufficient oversight and interagency cooperation, President Clinton set up the Vice President's Community Empowerment Board along with the Departments of Housing and Urban Development and Agriculture to oversee implementation of the President's Empowerment Zones and Enterprise Communities Program. As part of the strategic planning process, communities will have to address the level of drug abuse and drug-related activity in their communities through the expansion of drug treatment services, drug law enforcement initiatives, and community-based drug abuse education and prevention programs.

President Clinton's 1994 Strategy called for resources to empower communities to confront their drug problems directly. A total of $1 billion was requested for community based efforts. $50 million of this figure was earmarked for the drug related demand side of the Community Empowerment Program. This program is designed to provide residential and nonresidential drug and alcohol prevention and treatment programs that offer comprehensive services for pregnant women as well as mothers and their children.

## Community Policing

One of President Clinton's most important law enforcement goals, the reduction of domestic crime and violence, is designed to make the Nation's communities — particularly those hit hardest by drug abuse and drug-related crime — once again safe and free from the fear that the drug industry creates. To make the Nation's streets safer, President Clinton passed a tough and smart crime bill.

The key part of the Crime Bill was designed to put more police on the streets over a five year period and to expand the community policing concept. More cops on the beat is a integral part of something called community policing. Community policing seeks to move away from reactive 911 policing and toward a more proactive approach to law enforcement (Moore, 1994).

The cop on the beat can work with other neighborhood leaders in helping to solve the grass roots causes of drug abuse. To enable this to happen, $568 million of the $1 billion community empowerment money was slated for the drug component of the plan to put more "cops on the beat." The original plan was to put over 100,000 more police officers on the street over a five year period to work with communities to reduce crime — a nationwide increase of 16 percent. The program was intended to rehire laid off police officers and to hire new police officers.

The program provides funds for specialized training of police officers to enhance their problem-solving, conflict resolution, mediation, and other skills and to work in partnership with the community. They can then interact more effectively with community residents, who in turn are actively encouraged to assist police officers in creative crime prevention. The program also includes innovative crime control and prevention programs involving young people and police officers in the community.

One of the most appealing aspects of community policing is its ability to use community engagement and problemsolving to reduce both the supply of and demand for drugs and thereby minimize the negative consequences of drug trafficking and abuse. More police on the street working in partnership with community residents means less crime and less fear of crime. In this way, communities can reclaim their parks, playgrounds and streets. Moreover, by reducing the demand for drugs as well as discouraging all forms of criminal behavior, community policing promotes community cohesion, which is essential to developing effective community-based drug treatment and prevention programs.

Law enforcement agencies must maintain their commitment to help these neighborhoods contain and reduce drug use and respond to the problems it creates. Once the required mutual trust is established between the community and police department, the benefits of such programs are both mutual and cumulative. Police officers receive more complete and timely information on crimes and criminals. They also engender a sense of community purpose and well-being and the community rids itself of those who would intimidate and harm it.

The Clinton administration's community policing program also helps to develop new administrative and managerial systems that facilitate the adoption of community policing as a department wide philosophy. In this regard, the program offers new technology to assist police departments in reorienting the emphasis of their activities from reacting to crime to preventing crime. It also increases police participation in early multi-agency intervention programs.

More cops on the beat and community policing help to make streets safer through more creative law enforcement and community action. But a community is more than safe streets. Successful and desirable communities also enjoy safe and prosperous drug-free workplaces. Therefore, one of President Clinton's goals is to increase workplace safety and productivity by reducing drug use in the workplace. If successful, this effort could save the Nation billions of dollars in lost productivity, health care, etc. The goal calls for increased employee counseling through Employee Assistance Programs (EAP). However, businesses are encouraged rather than directed to establish such programs. Frankly, unless Congress gives employers something more tangible, the goal will probably not be reached anytime soon. Community actions teams must work with local businesses to increase the funding for this worthwhile activity.

Attractive communities also enjoy safe and drug free schools. President Clinton has done his part in creating a program designed to create safe and healthy schools where children and adolescents can live, grow, learn and develop. Part of the program is to expand the number of public schools that afford safe areas for children after school and on weekends. But the overall thrust of the program is dedicated to improving the education and prevention programs in schools across the country.

As cited earlier, recent surveys of young people's attitudes and behavior about illegal drugs show that the long-term decline in drug use among youth has ended. After declining for almost a decade in the 1980s, teen-age drug use is on the rise in the 1990s. The annual Monitoring the Future survey released on December 15, 1995 found that teen-age drug use has risen steadily since 1992.

Take marijuana for example. Marijuana use by eighth graders has nearly doubled since 1991, with nearly 20 percent of these students reporting that they have used it at least once. That's up from 17 percent just one year earlier. Similarly, more than 48 percent of high school seniors in the class of 1995 had used some type of illegal drug at least once, up almost 3 percentage points from 1994 (The Sentinel, (1995), December 16, p. a3). In addition, recent studies report that there is an alarming level of violence that accompanies this drug use in and around our schools.

While the overall thrust of President Clinton's Safe and Drug Free Schools and Communities (SDFSC) program is designed to prevent children and adolescents from getting hooked on illegal drugs, President Clinton is also seeking to reduce the use of alcohol and tobacco products among underage youth. This goal makes a lot of sense since alcohol and tobacco kill more Americans than any combination of illegal drugs. The objective is to increase prevention and education so as to reverse the increase of drug use, alcohol and tobacco among students. It is admittedly ambitious. But it also noble and absolutely necessary.

Congress as cited earlier is openly opposing President Clinton's efforts to reverse the trend of increased drug use in schools. The House wants to cut about 60 % of the requested SDFSC funds for FY 1996. If House cuts stick, this House action would adversely affect 97 % of the Nation's public schools at a time when drug use by children and adolescents is going up across the country (ONDCP, 1995). As money dries up in Washington, embattled communities will have to find other ways to fund these worthwhile programs in the future. The lessons learned from the Cafe 458 case study cited earlier should not be forgotten. But it's wrong to assume that even strong grass-roots programs can make it totally on their own. The U.S. government must care and be involved.

Some of the public policy difficulties over drug prevention stem from too much of the overall National Drug Control drug control pie being wasted on futile supply side programs and not enough on more cost effective demand side programs. While Congress deserves the lion's share of the blame for the lopsided policies in recent years, President Clinton is also responsible. In his February 1995 National Drug Control Strategy, President Clinton actually moved away from efforts to beef up demand side reduction. President Clinton increased the percentage of the total drug control budget for supply reduction from 62.8 percent to 63.9 percent (White House Budget, 1995, p. 23).

What explains President Clinton's policy reversal on drug control strategy? Nobody knows for sure what caused President Clinton to abandon his early convictions supporting a strong shift to demand reduction. But one thing is certain. Those supporters of the Clinton administration who looked for strong Presidential support for their demand side reduction efforts are noticeably frustrated by President Clinton's movement away from demand side priorities.

Aware that a strong shift to demand side reduction could possibly be a political liability on the campaign trail, President Clinton may want to appear "tougher" than the Republicans on Capital Hill in trying to reduce the supply of drugs (White House, pp. 22-23). This could also be a reason for selecting a "tough" military man like General Barry McCaffrey to be the new Drug Czar.

But two can play this game. With $700 million of the $1 billion in proposed congressional cuts coming from demand side programs, the Republican controlled Congress is now trying to increase the share of the pie going to supply side programs by another 2 percent. Instead of Clinton's 64 perecent or so for supply reduction, Republicans in Congress can now say they want to spend 66 percent (or 2 percent more than Clinton) in reducing the supply of drugs.

Somehow the funding shortfall for demand side programs must be overcome. One way is to simply try to divert money from ineffective supply side programs to more promising demand side programs. But this shift is politically difficult as cited above. It is also difficult in a procedural sense on Capital Hill given the fact that there are nine Congressional appropriation committees which control bits and pieces of the drug control budget pie. Convincing one appropriation committee to spend less on the supply side is no guarantee that this money will be spent on demand reduction programs. The money could be used instead for programs that have nothing to do with drug policy. The money could also be used as savings to lower the budget deficit. Congressional reorganization could help. But this is not likely anytime soon.

On the other hand, the prevention challenge is not simply a question of where the money is coming from to fund programs. Increases in federal or local funding are not enough. Two years of data show that the standard prevention message is getting stale. Scare tactics and "just say no" messages simply miss the mark with large sections of the Nation's rebellious youth for a variety of reasons. We therefore must improve the quality of today's prevention message. This means more analysis is needed to determine what works and what doesn't work in dissuading children and adolescents from taking drugs.

But before Madison Avenue can help us develop a better way to connect to the today's youth, we need to step back and ask more fundamental questions. In the next chapter we will explore the available medical and scientific literature to discover why so many Americans take drugs and why some of these people get addicted and others do not. This inquiry is a necessary first step before we can implement what works and what doesn't in the prevention area. Only then will we all be able to move beyond the Clinton Strategy and develop more secure footing for responsible public policy on drug abuse.

## References

Buckley, W., (1993), "From the Battlefront," *National Review*, March 1.

Douglas, J., (1993), "U.S. is Cutting Aid to Latin Drug War," *New York Times*. March 25.

Dryfoos, J., (1993), "Preventing Substance Abuse: Rethinking Strategies," *American Journal of Public Health*, June 1993, Zuckerman, M. (1993) "Fighting the Right Drug War," *U.S. Garr, R. 1995, Reinvesting in America. News and World Report*, April 26.

Kramer, M., (1994), "From Sarajevo to Needle Park," *Time*, February 21.

Labaton, S., (1993), "Reno Questions Drug Policy's Stress on Smuggling," *New York Times*, May 8.

Moore, M., (1994), *Beyond 911*.

*New York Times*, (1993), "Mr. Clinton's Invisible Drug Policy," editorial, April 22.

*New York Times*, (1993), "Military's Drug Interdiction is Labeled a Failure," September 16.

Portner, J., (1993), "Drug Cuts Passed by House Shock Prevention Advocates," *Education Week*, August 4.

Treaster, J., (1993), "Pentagon Plans Shift in War on Drug Traffickers," *New York Times*, October 29.

*U.S. News and World Report*, (1993), "Clinton's Shift in the War on Drugs," September 27.

The White House, (1993b), Statement by the Press Secretary on PDD-14 and the International Drug Policy.

The White House, (1994), *National Drug Control Strategy*, February.

# 6  Beyond the Clinton Strategy

If drugs are so destructive, you might think that this sober reality would be enough to dissuade most people from using drugs in the first place. And yet we know the standard education and prevention message – while an essential first line of defense — is not sufficient and is getting stale. This being the case, we need to explore why Americans use illegal drugs and abuse legal drugs even when the risks are known, taking into account factors which have not been adequately considered by any previous administration.

No study of drugs in American society would be complete without citing briefly the marketing of drug use. Whether we are talking about legal or illegal drugs, it is important to remember that they are not simply used. Drugs are bought and sold in huge amounts, and the economic force behind the marketing of both legal and illegal drugs is truly enormous. Consider the legal drug enterprises. The alcoholic beverage industry earns billions of dollars at the retail level in the United States each year. Billions of dollars are also spent each year on tobacco products, pharmaceutical, and over-the-counter medications.

Sales of this magnitude don't just happen. Madison Avenue aggressively advertises legal drugs at every turn. Television and radio commercials tell viewers or listeners that if you don't feel good, pop a pill. If you want to feel really good, drink a beer. And while tobacco advertising is more restricted these days, the alluring message of smoking is not missed by impressionistic teenagers. Meanwhile, over-worked physicians in America are frequently easy prey for the pharmaceutical houses' "drug reps" and their relentless sales tactics. This Madison Avenue "quick thrill" assault has turned America into a pill culture.

Conditioned by this pill culture, it is all too easy for otherwise well-adjusted Americans to "get hooked" and abuse legal or illegal drugs. And as part of a pill culture, many teenage Americans reject the distinction their parents make between illegal and legal drugs as non-persuasive and at times hypocritical. And since legal drugs (such as alcohol and tobacco) kill far more Americans than illegal drugs, it is easy enough for teenage Americans to rationalize their decision to seek quick thrills with illegal drugs. While the size of the illegal drug industry is more difficult to determine than the legal drug industry, it is fair to say that the marketing of illegal drugs is just as aggressive and relentless and insidious as legal marketing.

Of course, it would be misleading to conclude that Americans are unique when it comes to using drugs. After all, the use of drugs has been a feature of human life in all places on the earth and throughout history. And today, more than 95 percent of Americans use some form of mind-altering substance. In fact, Americans are continuously struggling with the right relationship with these substances (see Diamond, 1987; Perry, 1990; *Newsweek*, 1990, May and Goldstein, 1986). In almost all cases, people take drugs for the obvious reason that they like what drugs do to them, which is to induce alterations in consciousness. Ronald Siegel argues that the motivation to achieve an altered state of mood or consciousness is a "fourth drive", as much a part of the human condition as sex, thirst and hunger (see Siegal, 1989).

Siegel's research shows that this basic and universal urge for people to get high is also found in the animal kingdom. In the Andes, llamas, birds, snails and insects as well as people all consume cocaine by eating leaves or seeds from the coca plant. In the Canadian Rockies, bighorn sheep grind their teeth to the gums nibbling at a narcotic lichen that grows on bare rocks. In the Texas desert, goats and pack horses eat the hallucinogenic mescal beans even though the beans lack usable nutrients. Water buffalo eat opium poppies and even robins get high by gorging themselves on ripening firethorn and toyon berries. However, while a basic and universal drive to get high may exist in people and animals, Andrew Weil reminds us that the desire to alter consciousness need not be achieved by means of chemical agents. Weil maintains that drugs are merely one means of satisfying this drive. Of course, many other means exist as well.

Any child who has ever spun round and round into a dizzy stupor knows a drug-free high. So do African natives who perform ritual dances. Committed joggers are sometimes so devoted to their daily "runner's high" that many injure themselves through overtraining. When ordered by a doctor to stop, they often display such symptoms of withdrawal as irritability, nervousness and loss of concentration.

Since the 1970s, medical researchers who study the runner's high and other natural alterations in consciousness have zeroed in on a group of internally generated mood-control agents known as endogenous morphines, or endorphins (see Hopson, 1988). These natural bodily created substances are believed to play a key role in determining whether we are anxious or relaxed, unable to concentrate or immersed in thought. They are chemically related to forbidden exogenous opiates such as opium, morphine and heroin, and produce a similar psychological state – a sense of bliss, floating and transcendence of ego.

Interestingly enough, you do not have to run or engage in vigorous physical exercise for your body to experience these internally generated endorphins. Charles F. Levinthal, in his book *Messengers of Paradise: Opiates and the Brain*, discusses

70

how doctors speak of being addicted to their work (see Levinthal, 1996). One surgeon said operating was "like taking narcotics" and another compared it to heroin. In the words of Daniel Lazare,

> For centuries, people who have spoken of "losing" themselves in their work, of shutting out the world while they concentrate on an intellectual problem, may actually have [been] describing a heightened mental state brought on by an internally generated drug. They may not be so much devoted to their profession as devoted to a chemical high that scientists now believe may be brought on by hard work or vigorous physical exercise (see Lazare, 1989)

But if all of us may be hooked in one way or another on the urge to get high, the consequences are entirely different for the heroin addict who shoots up than for the surgeon, the long distance runner, or for the water buffalo that eats opium poppies. In the case of water buffalo, the natural packaging of opium effectively prohibits harmful doses. Similarly, the long distance runner and the surgeons are in no danger from their self-generated drug-free highs.

But the heroin addict is a different story. His use is a form of self-poisoning and he is dependent on outside sources to satisfy his opiate craving. Either he has never learned to generate his own natural high, or he lacks the discipline or training to do what a long distance runner does. Instead, he is too lazy or too impatient to be bothered with generating a natural high and so he takes big risks for his quick fix. Sadly, he depends for his potentially life threatening high on someone messing around with Mother Nature and concentrating the dose of what the water buffalo ate relatively harmlessly for its high.

### How Americans Get Hooked On Drugs

Now that we have some sense of the "animal instinct" theory of why Americans decide to take drugs, we need to ask ourselves what happens to people who start to "fool around" with them. Well meaning parents sometimes warn their children that drug use inevitably leads to addiction. While this pitch is understandable it is also inaccurate, and not helpful in the treatment of people who want to stop using drugs. While research on adolescents shows that their involvement with drugs progresses in a characteristic pattern, with the use of one class of drugs generally acting as "a gateway" or progression to other substances, addiction is certainly not inevitable for each and everyone who experiments with drugs (Kandel, 1975, pp. 912-914; and Califano, 1994)

Similarly, the view that one is either an abstainer or an addict has no basis in fact. Drug use is a continuum, not an either-or proposition.

71

Experimentation does not necessarily lead to regular use, and regular use does not necessarily lead to compulsive use or addiction. For every drug, it is possible to find users at every point along the spectrum – from experimentation to occasional use to regular use to outright addiction. There is no inevitable "slide" from less to more involved levels of use (see Goode, 1989, pp. 46-52; and Goleman, 1989).

To understand how some people become physically dependent on (or addicted to) drugs while others do not, we first need to study the characteristic of the drug. That in turn will tell us about the biological or biochemical basis for addiction. All drugs – legal or illegal – possess characteristics unique to themselves that influence how and how often they are used. In terms of addiction (or physical dependence) it is critical to understand how "reinforcing" drugs (such as heroin, amphetamines and cocaine) are extremely pleasurable in an immediate sense and possess a high addiction potential. Conversely, drugs like alcohol, marijuana and hallucinogens are less reinforcing, with the pleasure being less immediate, more diluted, less sensuous and more of an acquired taste. As a result, these less reinforcing drugs have a lower addiction potential.

But the characteristic of the drug is not sufficient to explain addiction. Another critical factor is how a drug is taken (or its route of administration). Some methods of use (such as injection and smoking) are highly reinforcing, with the pleasure being immediate and highly sensuous. Conversely, other methods of use (oral and nasal) are slower, less reinforcing techniques, with the effects of the drugs being slower, more muted and less immediately sensuous.

If we couple these two factors (the characteristics of the drug and the mechanism of its use) it is clear that whenever a highly reinforcing drug is taken in a highly reinforcing fashion, its addiction potential is large. Conversely, if a less immediately pleasurable drug is taken in a less reinforcing fashion, its addiction potential is far smaller. That being the case, it is easy to see why heroin, crack and injected cocaine are likely to generate a high proportion of addicts (see Marsi, 1989; Holloway, 1991; Booth, 1990; Kanigel, 1988; and Pekkanen, 1984).

The assumption that drug addiction can be understood in terms of the pharmacologic properties of certain drugs has given rise to a number of biological theories of drug abuse. These theories have in turn focused on the concept of physical dependence and the idea that drug abuse is a compulsive, uncontrollable behavior aimed at temporary alleviation of withdrawal symptoms and the satisfaction of a physical need (see Wise, 1987, pp. 469-492; Kozlowski, 1991, pp. 517-520; and Gottheil, 1983).

According to most biological theories of drug abuse, continued drug use reduces an individual's sensitivity to a given drug. As insensitivity develops, the individual requires increasingly higher doses to obtain the same pharmacologic effect. If the individual should decide to reduce or stop the drug, unpleasant physical withdrawal symptoms can result, often leading to the resumption of drug use. These withdrawal symptoms vary considerably depending on the type of drug (Herson, 1977, pp. 953-971). However, for drugs such as alcohol, opiates and barbiturates, physiological signs of withdrawal include cramps, nausea and sweating.

Overall, biological theories of drug abuse and its key concept of physical dependence may partially account for habitual drug use. But these biological theories do little to explain initial drug use, or for that matter the mechanisms by which some people develop drug dependence whereas others do not. In other words, why is it that one person can use a highly reinforcing drug in a highly reinforcing fashion and get addicted while another person can do the same thing and not get hooked? To answer this question we may want to reassess the earlier idea that the urge to alter one's consciousness is a basic and universal human drive. Notwithstanding self-generated endorphins, a number of drug researchers disagree with Bob Dylan's phrase, "Everybody Must Get Stoned."

In fact, some people in America and elsewhere are lifetime abstainers. Others use drugs like alcohol and tobacco moderately and, arguably, responsibly. And still others are psychologically dependent or physically addicted to drugs. In other words, the "animal instinct" theory of Weil and Siegel fails to address the variability of drug use among Americans and other people. So we need to explore differences among individuals (see Franklyn, 1990 and Schuckit, 1982).

If we assume that we are all different, then maybe we should explore a possible genetic basis to drug addiction. Perhaps some people are simply born with a genetic propensity to abuse, and become physically dependent on addictive drugs. For this reason, additional research has focused on the identification of biological characteristics that may be associated with an increased vulnerability to heavy drug use. While no conclusive or widely accepted marker of a biological predisposition to drug abuse has been discovered, considerable evidence implicates genetic factors in the transmission of some forms of drug dependence, particularly alcoholism (see Holden, 1991; McCue, 1992, pp. 3-17; Bohman, 1981, pp. 965-969; Hrubeck, 1981 and Goodwin, 1973, pp. 238-243). In this regard, the so-called dopamine D2 receptor gene is associated with alcoholism. A study by Kenneth Blum of the University of Texas Health Science Center and Ernest Noble from UCLA published in the April 1990 *Journal of the American Medical Association* suggests that this gene confers susceptibility to at least one form of alcoholism (see Blum, 1990).

People with this gene may have an unusual insensitivity to the effects of alcohol which would cause them to drink in excess and feel only slightly drunk when in fact they are very drunk. This slightly drunk feeling in turn influences them to drink more than others do. The genetic work of Blum and other researchers is beginning to help identify at-risk population groupings; in particular, it is strengthening the evidence implicating genetic factors in the transmission of alcoholism. For example, the rate of alcoholism among identical twins appears significantly higher than the rate of alcoholism among fraternal twins (see Brubeck,

1981; Wheeler, 1987).

Similarly, the prevalence of alcohol problems among adopted-away children of alcoholics is greater than the prevalence of such problems among the adopted-away children of nonalcoholics. And the adopted sons of alcoholics had higher rates of subsequent alcoholism than did a control group composed of the adopted sons of nonalcoholic (Goodwin, 1973, pp. 238-243). But it is important not to make sweeping conclusions based on the above research. For instance, other research suggests that the inherited risk of alcoholism is substantial only for certain subtypes of male alcoholics, and that other subtypes may be more responsive to nonbiological factors (Cloninger, 1981, pp. 861-868). But could the correlation between specific genes and certain kinds of alcoholism be extended to other kinds of drug addictions? The research of Neuroscientist Henri Begleiter of SUNY's Health Science Center at Brooklyn suggests that there may be genes for compulsive disease in general. Beigleiter says low levels of platelet monoamine oxidase (MAO) have long been suspected to be related to alcoholism, but it now seems they may correlate better to compulsive disorders in general. He has found anomalies in the brainwaves of both the young sons of alcoholics and in those of cocaine abusers.

Still other researchers, while open to the idea of a general susceptibility explanation, continue to place an emphasis on the possibility that there are genes specific to alcoholism. For example, Kenneth Blum believes that there may be genes for "compulsive disease" as well as subgenes (or modifier genes) that dictate susceptibilities to particular substances (Holden, 1991, pp. 163-164).

Overall, the research indicates that genetic factors are associated with drug abuse particularly alcoholism (Goodwin, 1985, pp. 171-174). But considerable uncertainty exists with respect to the nature and extent of this link and the mechanisms by which it operates. Moreover, while physiological dependence and a genetic predisposition to addiction plays some role in drug abuse, the contribution of biological factors to casual or experimental drug use is less clear. Most importantly, the research on the genetic and biological factors associated – however incomplete – with drug abuse is important in the sense that it conditions how health officials deal with drug addicts. In fact, health officials tend to work under the assumption that drug addicts have physiological differences from normal people, differences based in a genetic source and/or created through the use of the drugs. In other words, most professionals who treat drug addicts assume their patients have a disease.

James R. Milam and Katherine Ketcham, authors of *Under the Influence* (1981) are popular advocates of this disease model to explain why people get hooked on alcohol (see Milan, 1981). Similarly, Mark S. Gold argues that cocaine addicts also suffer from a disease. Crucial to the disease model is the idea that the user loses control; the drug itself and physiological changes in the addict's body are said to control further ingestion of drugs. Thus, an involuntary process or a biochemical chain reaction starts and the addict is said to have an uncontrollable physical demand for more drugs (see Schaler, 1981). Notice that this disease model of drug addiction is mechanistic in that the interaction between physiology and the chemicals in the drug are viewed as both the disease and the executor of behavior and experience. The drug addict is therefore viewed as a machine that is broken.

In his 1989 book *The Diseasing of America*, Stanton Peele discusses how the disease model is being used to absolve drug users of any responsibility or accountability for their actions (see Peele, 1989 and Charen, 1989). Jeffrey A. Schaler explains the logic of this shoddy practice:

> Drug use constitutes an addiction. Addiction is a disease. Acts stemming from the disease are called symptoms. Since the symptoms of a disease are involuntary, the symptoms of drug addiction disease are likewise involuntary. Addicts are thus not responsible for their actions (Schaler, 1991).

The abuse of this disease model was apparent to most people after Marion Barry, Mayor of Washington D.C., was videotaped buying cocaine. His defense was "that it was the disease talking . . . I was a victim." It was the disease of drug addiction that allegedly forced him to use drugs. He was "powerless" in relation to drugs, his life was "unmanageable" and "out of control." (Schaler; Epstine, 1989).

The dubious nature of such a disease alibi is causing many people to question the whole disease model of how people get hooked on drugs. Certainly drug addiction is not analogous to real diseases such as diabetes, heart disease or cancer that are involuntary developments inside the body. Thomas Szasz, Professor of Psychiatry at SUNY Syracuse, reminds us that a disease is really a phenomenon limited to the body. He argues that it actually has no relationship to drug use. Szasz disagrees with the disease model of addiction on the basis of the distinction between behavior and disease. In *Insanity: The Idea and Its Consequences* (1987) he states:

> [B]y behavior we mean the person's 'mode of conducting himself' or his 'deportment' . . . the name we attach to a living being's conduct in the daily pursuit of life . . . [B]odily movements that are the products of neurophysiological discharges or reflexes are not behavior . . . The point is that behavior implies action, and action implies conduct pursued by an agent seeking to attain a goal (Szaxz, 1987).

The questionable practice of constantly using the disease model to absolve the drug addict of any responsibility or accountability has given rise to a moralistic model of drug addiction. This moralistic model has its historical roots in the temperance movement that evolved into national prohibition in 1920. According to this model, addiction results from low moral standards, bad character and weak will. Addicts are viewed as bad people who have "sinned" and they lack basic human values. To some extent, this model is consistent with the Bush Administration's view. When President Bush was asked how to solve the drug problem during the televised debates of the 1988 presidential campaign, the president said "by instilling values" (see Schaler).

How should we assess the disease model and the moralistic model? The disease model may be useful for people with extreme forms of alcoholism or other drug addictions. But for many people with moderate forms of addiction, the model is probably not appropriate. On the other hand, the moralistic model may be valuable in calling for higher moral standards. But is it fair to punish a moderate drinker who gradually becomes an alcoholic? And while some would make a distinction here between legal and illegal drug addiction, that distinction is as irrelevant to people who abuse drugs as the 55 m.p.h. speed limit was to most motorists. We have also seen that the urge to get high is natural, not immoral. What is missing for the addict is a control mechanism.

On balance, the disease model is useful in some respects, but it fails to adequately explain many features of the drug scene. For instance, why are there so many alcoholics, given the fact that the drug is nearly always taken in a less reinforcing fashion? The answer to this question and many others clearly cannot be explained by only studying a biological or biochemical basis for physical dependence (or addiction). If we therefore assume that the variability of drug use among individuals is not only – or maybe even primarily – genetic, then perhaps we should explore behavioral factors to get a fuller explanation of drug abuse. Perhaps we need to ask different kinds of questions. For instance, what types of people get hooked on drugs? And why do some individuals become impulsive and destructive in their drug use while others who use these drugs do not behave in this way? Are different drugs appealing to different personality types?

The behavioral model is the third and the most persuasive way of helping to explain how Americans get hooked on drugs. In contrast to the disease model of a helpless drug addict overpowered by disease, behavioralists attribute most forms of drug addiction to psychological and environmental factors. In this sense, drug use becomes more an intentional, voluntary way of goal seeking in order to cope with the perception of an adverse environment. The behavioral school is itself sub-divided into a number of intellectual camps, each with its own model of drug abuse.

Some of the behavioralists explain drug use as a function of an individual's personality characteristics. These drug users are attracted to their drugs of choice because of who they are and what their personalities find attractive. For instance, someone with low self-esteem might decide to abuse drugs for one reason while a person with poor coping and conflict skills might choose to abuse drugs for an entirely different reason (Frank, 1990, pp. 770-780; Cooper, 1992, pp. 139-152). Similarly, a British longitudinal study on mental health linked sensation seeking to drug use patterns (Pedersen, 1991, pp. 195-204). Another longitudinal study of alienation in the workplace linked perceived powerlessness to alcohol use. A study that explained delinquency and drug use and another explaining the origins of alcoholism both link early antisocial behavior and drug use (Seeman, 1988, pp. 185-198). An eight year study of multiple influences on drug use underscored the importance of social nonconformity as an important personality characteristic/behavior style in the explanation of drug use (Stein, 1987, pp. 1094-1105). And finally, a longitudinal study of adolescent drug use shows how psychological dysfunction can be implicated in drug abuse (Shedler, 1990, pp. 612-630).

After Craig Nakken published his book entitled *The Addictive Personality: Understanding Compulsion in Our Lives*, (Nakken, *Newsweek*, 1989), many behavioralists hoped to discover an "addictive personality" (with consistent personality characteristics and behavior styles) that was somehow common to all heavy drug abusers. But despite the popularity and simplicity of the addictive personality concept, serious research did not support this notion. Personality characteristics and behavior styles of the heavy drug users simply seemed too diverse for an addictive personality model. But then in 1990, Shedler and Block published an article that has revived interest in at least the popular concept of an addictive personality and drug abuse (Shedler, 1990, pp. 612-630).

In their definitive longitudinal study of psychological health and subsequent adolescent drug use, Shedler and Block found that the personality characteristics of frequent drug users differed from nonusers and casual users. Most importantly, these differences were evident from early childhood, predating drug use. In contrast with occasional drug users, frequent drug users were described as emotionally and socially maladjusted (Donovan, 1985, pp. 890-904). The Shedler and Block article has increased the interest in the personal history of drug addicts. Generally speaking, these researchers are finding that drug abusers experienced an unhappy childhood. Before taking drugs they were lonely, sad and frightened people who never felt they belonged. Because of this potentially fatal personality flaw, they simply lacked the basic psychological equipment to cope with a dismal existence (Stein, 1988).

In contrast to a relatively well adjusted person who may sample recreational drugs and then quit, the drug addict discovers that drugs boost his ego and make him feel like he belongs to something for the first time. Whether the drug is legal or illegal is immaterial. The point is that the drugs change the person's relation to the universe, offering a crutch that organizes his life. For awhile he truly believes that his life would be unbearable without drugs. In other words, a drug addict finds that drugs fill an emptiness and make him feel whole.

While this addictive personality model is gaining more interest since the Shedler and Block article, other behavioral researchers prefer the cognitive and social learning model of drug abuse (Wilson, 1987, pp. 325-331). In this model one's beliefs about the consequences of drug use influence subsequent involvement with drugs. G. Alan Marlatt of the University of Washington at Seattle agrees that it is expectations and beliefs about a drug's power to make one feel better that shape the choices of the addictive personality that lead to drug abuse (Bower, 1988). In fact, the evidence is quite persuasive that acquired attitudes and beliefs about the consequences of drug use do play a role in determining the amount of drug use in America. For instance, surveys have shown that drug users generally believe that drugs relieve tension, promote well-being and enhance interpersonal comfort (Chritchlow, 1986, pp. 751-764; Leigh, 1989, pp. 361-373). G. Alan Marlatt contends that the most notable of these beliefs is that alcohol acts as a psychological and social lubricant that enhances pleasure, increases sexual responsiveness and assertiveness and reduces tension (Bower, 1988). Interestingly enough, laboratory studies of alcohol use indicate that social anxiety is reduced among men who believed that they drank alcohol even if they had been administered a placebo (Wilson, 1977, pp. 195-210; Kine, 1988).

Other behavioralists view drug addicts more as people who unhappily developed "intoxicating habits" rather than addictive personalities. In other words, these drug users simply learned to do the wrong things with the substances they use and abuse. A central theme derived from behavioral learning models focuses on the gratifying consequences of drug use. Drug use is viewed as an acquired habit that is perpetuated by its reinforcing consequences, including changes in the psychological, emotional and physical well-being of the user (Levison, 1983). While the reinforcing consequence for cocaine is euphoria, the reinforcement for smoking (e.g., nicotine) may be either anxiety reduction or enhanced powers of concentration (Pomerleau, 1987, pp. 278-287; Rose, 1991, pp. 605-609; Nathan, 1985, pp. 141-158). In his book *Heavy Drinking: The Myth of Alcoholism as a Disease*, Herbert Fingarette argues that alcoholism is a learned behavior, not a disease. According to Fingarette, alcoholism has no single cause and has no medical cure. It results from his conception of intoxicating habits, which he defines as a whole range of personal and social characteristics that predispose a person to drink excessively (Finagrette, 1988).

A related behavioral learning model of drug use involves the role of situational or environmental cues that become associated with drug use over time, setting off an addict's craving or irresistible urge to use drugs. The user of the drug has simply learned to do the wrong things with the substances he uses and abuses. Just as Pavlov's dogs learned to salivate at the sound of a bell, the stimuli in the addict's environment serve as internal and external "bells" that provoke a craving in many users. Addicts associate these cues with pleasure because they have been associated with reinforcement in the past. Treatment is therefore premised on the idea that such associations can be unlearned as readily as they were learned.

Circumstances associated with drug use (such as a physical setting, a social setting, time of day or internal mental state) can themselves trigger drug use by repeated association with the reinforcing aspects of drug use. Over time, these situational or temporal correlates of drug use (such as physical or social setting or time of day) can serve as cues that promote drug abuse. These cues or bells are often quite specific. For example, in a survey of 150 former alcoholics reported in the Fall 1986 issue of *Alcohol Health and Research World*, Arnold M. Ludwig of the University of Kentucky Medical Center in Lexington compiled a list of drinking "bells" (Lunwig). These cues or mental bells included going to a dance, feeling lonely, having a barbecue and driving past former drinking hangouts. Interestingly enough, numerous studies suggest that the sensory characteristics of tobacco (such as its aroma) play a role in tobacco use even in the absence of nicotine intake (Abelin, 1989; Rose, 1991, pp. 605-609). In fact, similar studies have demonstrated that nicotine administration may have no influence on the craving for cigarettes (Fertig, 1986, pp. 239-248).

But this discussion of how cues or bells trigger drug use begs the question as to why do some people see these cues and still drastically cut back their drinking without formal treatment while others get hooked? Behavioralists who stress environmental factors argue that external events often conspire to change an individual's attitude toward alcohol. In other words, what goes on outside of a person's body is more significant in explaining drug addiction than what goes on inside the body (Schaler, 1991). Particularly important for military readers is a study commissioned by the Department of Defense led by epidemiologist Lee N. Robins. The study shows that only 14 percent of those who used heroin in Vietnam remained addicted after returning to the United States. These findings support the theory that drug use – even the use of heroin (long considered a physically addictive drug) – can be a function of environmental stress, which in this case ceased when the veterans left Vietnam. Soldiers said they used heroin to cope with the harrowing experiences of war (Robins 1975, pp. 955-961)..

As Robins and the co-authors state in *Archives of General Psychiatry*:

> [I]t does seem clear that the opiates are not so addictive that use is necessarily followed by addiction. Nor is it true that once addicted, an individual is necessarily addicted permanently. At least in certain circumstances, individuals can use narcotics regularly and even become addicted to them but yet be able to avoid use in other social circumstances . . . How generalizable these results are is currently unknown. No previous study has had so large and so unbiased a sample of heroin users (Robins)

Much of the debate over drug addiction centers around the question of how much free will a drug addict may or may not have. The research of Timothy B. Baker, a psychologist from the University of Wisconsin in Madison, supports a free will model of drug addiction (Bower, 1988, pp. 88-89). Baker argues that addiction really does not occur in the liver or in the genes. It is true that biology may in some cases increase a person's risk of developing a dependency, but Baker agrees with January 1992 former President Bush's *National Drug Control Strategy* view that says "the drug problem reflects bad decisions by individuals with free wills." (White House, 1992, p. 2).

Where Baker and President Bush disagree somewhat is over the environmental variables. Baker argues that addiction occurs in an environment. While an individual chooses to take drugs, Baker contends that the "likelihood of a person trying a drug or eventually becoming addicted is influenced by his or her friends, marital happiness, the variety and richness of alternatives to drug use and so on." (Bower, 1988, pp. 88-89; Bower, 1989, pp. 392-393). President Bush, on the other hand, argues that social conditions "victimize" drug users and "deprive them of personal autonomy – the freedom and will not to use drugs. It is to deny the dignity of those who live in similar circumstances and do not use drugs" (White House, 1992, p. 2). President Bush says drug use is not caused by poverty since most poor people do not use drugs. Nor is race involved since most minorities do not use drugs either and unemployment is not a factor since most of the jobless do not use drugs. President Bush also rejects the view that drug use can be at all associated with single parents, a teenage mother or with low educational attainment.

While President Bush emphasizes psychological factors, it is also true that ethnic and cultural groups do have different kinds of drug use. Some social groups seem to be more prone to drug abuse than others. Therefore an analysis of drug use and abuse would be incomplete without sociocultural perspectives. In this regard, Stanton Peele, a psychologist and health care researcher in Morris Plains, New Jersey, stresses the need to look closely at the influence of the society, the culture, social contexts or settings and sub-cultures within a given society on drug dependence (Peele, 1990, pp. 52-58). Certainly some categories in the population are more likely to use and abuse drugs than others. In short, it is incomplete and misleading to assume that sociological factors are not important.

What sociocultural factors are linked to drug use? The scholarly literature shows that low income, inner-city youth are more likely to engage in drug abuse and delinquency than are middle class or rural youth (Johnston, 1987). While the reasons for low income, inter-city youth being so prone to drug abuse are not altogether clear, lack of ties to school, church or other traditional support institutions is one possible factor (Elliott, 1989). Lack of achievement opportunities may be another aspect (Jessor, 1977). Other research notes additional factors that may influence drug abuse tendencies among different cultural, socioeconomic or religious groups. These factors include demographic and socioeconomic differences in beliefs about the harmful health effects of smoking, (Brownson, 1992, pp. 99-103) as well as differing cultural or religious values on drinking behavior (Engs, 1990, pp. 1475-1482; Burnam, 1987, pp. 89-102). Family and peer group characteristics are also associated with drug use. While it is true that the reinforcing effects of these drugs are mediated (or decreased) – at least in part – via neurobiological mechanisms, (Stellar, 1987, pp. 469-492), the reinforcing nature of non-biological factors such as enhanced social status and peer approval has been widely recognized in the literature. A study on middle class adolescents hospitalized for alcohol and other drug abuse indicated that their families were less cohesive and less emotionally supportive (Maltzman, 1991, pp. 1435-1447). In addition, a U.S. Department of Justice study on urban delinquency and drug abuse indicates that parental neglectfulness and other kinds of inadequate parenting heightens the risk of drug abuse (Huizinga, 1991). Similarly, research on early developmental factors finds that lax parental supervision increases the risk of alcohol abuse (Zucker, 1991, pp. 18-24).

All the research stresses the importance of a positive family structure in discouraging drug abuse. A number of studies show that adolescent smoking and other forms of drug use are greater in single parent households and among children of divorced parents (Goddard, 1992, pp. 17-18; Maltzman, 1991, pp. 1435-1447). And finally, a number of studies of adolescents indicate that parental, sibling and/or peer drug use contributes to adolescent drug use. Family and friends who use drugs act as role models, providers of access to drugs and approvers of drug use (Huba, 1979, pp. 265-271).

While Stanton Peele and former President Bush disagree over the importance of sociocultural variables, President Bush concedes that drug abuse is not solely a psychological or moral problem. The societal context is also important. "In the final analysis," President Bush argues, "the family must be the primary context in which we promote good health, morality, spiritual fulfillment, and the desire to achieve." (White House, 1992, p. 2). But while President Bush's emphasis on keeping the family together deserves applause, we must never ignore the huge number of people who are addicted to drugs and through no fault of their own are not part of a "Leave it to Beaver" family. We can not give up on drug addicts simply because they come from or live in broken or dysfunctional families.

## Different Perspectives On Drug Treatment

Now that we have a better understanding of drug use and abuse in America, we need to explore how U.S. society should attack the problem of drug abuse. Of all the drug-related issues, this one is arguably the most controversial. Let us look at our models of how people get hooked on drugs and explore whether or not these perspectives help us in the treatment of drug abusers.

The *moralist model* says America is losing the "war on drugs" because U.S. society is too permissive. Advocates of the moralist perspective argue that the U.S. government must be tougher on the users and dealers of illegal drugs, viewing the users of illegal drugs as "bad people" who need to be rehabilitated in "boot camps." Their drug-using behavior needs to be "punished" with harsh treatment. And so the moralist model is also a punitive model and is primarily coercive in its conversion approach. In many ways, the punitive nature of the Bush Administration's war on drugs with its call for "user accountability" reflected this moralistic perspective. President Reagan's zero tolerance approach was also consistent with this model. Since the moralistic model advocates feel justified in coercing these "bad people" into treatment, the model is paternalistic in its approach (Schaler, 1991, pp. 42-49).

But the moralists see drug treatment as only a part – and some would say too small a part – of an overall policy against drugs. What other kinds of policies does the coercive approach call for? The punitive approach tries to "solve" the drug problem with tougher laws, more arrests, longer jail and prison terms for drug offenders. It also calls for more police, more lethal police weapons, more interception of drugs smuggled into the country from abroad, more surveillance and fewer constitutional rights for dealers, users, and suspects. And finally, this coercive approach demands more planes, faster boats, more and bigger seizures of drug dealers' assets, more pressure on the governments of countries from which drugs originate, perhaps even the assistance of the armed forces (Schaler, 1981).

Another perspective which fell mainly outside the scope of this study is the *decriminalization or legalization model*. This perspective is diametrically opposed to the punitive model and starts with the premise that most of the problems of illegal drugs can be boiled down to economics or the profit motive. If illegal drugs were no longer profitable to sell, then the violence, corruption and medical problems associated with drug abuse would wither away. If so, the solution is clear enough — eliminate the laws against the possession, sale and use of drugs (Lazare, 1988; Jonas, 1990; Wilson, 1990).

The *disease model* rejects the premise of the other two models – that illegal drug abuse can be attacked by making the laws either tougher or more permissive. It argues that Americans who abuse drugs – legal or illegal – suffer from compulsive, self-destructive behavior. They are sick people who need help. Normally, that help would come in the form of medical treatment. The disease model advocates argue that addicts should not be punished for being sick and that treatment should focus on the biological factors that allegedly cause or reinforce drug use (Schaler, 1991, pp. 42-49). Note how different this disease model is from the moralistic model. Moralists reject the idea that drug addiction is a medical disease, and consider addiction to be the result of low moral standards. Treatment consists of punishment for the perpetrator. It is designed to deter the user from ever getting hooked again as well as to deter others from getting addicted.

Finally, the *behavioralists* have given us a totally different and more persuasive perspective from the moralists, legalizers or the disease model advocates. While we have seen that behavioralists can be sub-divided into a number of different camps, they all reject the moralistic and disease models of drug abuse. The behavioralists do not see drug abuse as a sin, a crime or a disease. Like it or not, behavioralists argue that drug abuse is a central activity of an individual's way of life. Seen in this context, treatment for drug abusers must not just focus on the drug problem per se. It must deal with the needs of the whole person as we saw at Cafe 458 in Atlanta. It must focus on developing a satisfying way of life that does not revolve around drug abuse (Hanson, 1990).

Behavioralists differentiate between well adjusted people and psychologically vulnerable people. While a well adjusted person might experiment with drugs, he invariably does not get hooked. In contrast, the psychologically vulnerable person is far more prone to drug addiction. Many experienced an unhappy childhood. Before taking drugs they were lonely, sad and frightened people who never felt they belonged. Because of this potentially fatal psychological flaw, they simply lacked the psychological equipment to cope with a dismal environment.

In contrast to the well adjusted person who samples drugs and then quits, the drug addict discovers that drugs boost his ego and make him feel like he belongs to something for the first time. It changes his relation to the universe. For awhile he truly believes his life would be unbearable without drugs. In other words, a drug addict finds that drugs fill an emptiness and make him feel whole (Schaler, 1991, pp. 42-49). At some point, however, the drug addict discovers that the negative effects of the habit are more dangerous than whatever meaningless life he had before he got hooked. As Benjamin Stein points out:

> He finds that sleepless nights, car crashes, nights in jail, loss of family, loss of job, loss of self-respect, loss of home are worse than what he had before. In other words, the drug has lost its ability to put the addict back into one piece again. The drug addiction has made him far more shattered than he ever was before he began to get high. (Stein, 1988, p. 6).

Behavioralists argue that at this point the drug addict is open to positive external intervention and drug treatment. Some would say that the drug abuser is open to an alternative "positive addiction." (see Glassner, 1976). This positive addiction may come from an understanding family that explains how the drug addict can swap long distance running or meditation for drug use (Sheehan 1980; Sheehan, 1978). Most of all, it gives the addict the opportunity to pursue a meaningful life that is arguably better than either the drug addictive life or the meaningless life he abandoned to take drugs in the first place.

What kind of drug treatment facility is the most successful in getting drug addicted Americans to abandon their compulsive, destructive behavior? Unfortunately, not enough is known about the outcome of various treatment programs to say definitely which one works best (Malcolm, 1989). But there are a number of different perspectives on drug treatment facilities that are competing for acceptance. The first perspective assumes that addicts cannot shake the drug habit unless they are physically removed from the environment which gives them the freedom to self-destruct. To get well, addicts live for an extended period of time in a therapeutic community where they are purged of the impulses that caused them to abuse drugs in the first place (Malcolm). For some drug abusers, these therapeutic communities are quite successful. But these communities require a sizeable investment of resources, and not all addicts who go to a therapeutic community emerge back into society changed people. Many leave these therapeutic communities prematurely and return to society with their addiction intact.

Some critics of therapeutic communities believe that treatment programs based on the Alcoholics Anonymous (AA) model are less expensive and are a more realistic alternative. The addicts remain in their natural environment but meet with other addicts and supervisors on a regular basis, sharing feelings about their compulsive behavior patterns with one another. Alcoholics Anonymous teaches that four general conditions — hunger, anger, loneliness, and tiredness – make alcoholics more vulnerable to drinking urges. If an alcoholic is to recover from his addiction, he must become aware of his own emotional and situational cues that trigger drinking urges. Then he must seek out "safehavens" where drinking is discouraged such as workplaces or outdoor activities. The same holds true for other addicts (Bower, 1988, pp. 88-89; Robertson, 1988).

Critics of the AA model argue that the programs only attract people who voluntarily decide to seek help, leaving lots of drug abusers untouched. Therefore, a number of drug observers think that drug abusers need to be threatened with a jail or prison term in order to force them into a mandatory treatment program. Regardless of whether drug abusers are forced to go for treatment or go on their own volition, there remains the problem of many long-term, hard-core addicts that are physically as well as psychologically hooked on drugs. For them, behavior modification is simply not enough. For long-term, hard-core heroin addicts, methadone maintenance may be the only viable program.

On the other hand, for lots of drug abusers, physical dependence or addiction is not the problem. They are trapped in an environment that encourages or at least condones their psychological dependence on drugs. While a therapeutic community may not be a necessary or practical alternative for these people, nonetheless the environment in which the drug abusers live – including friends, family and employment – has to be changed before their drug use can be addressed.

One of the most heated debates among people who treat alcoholics and other drug addicts revolves around the ultimate goal of the treatment. For instance, should the goal be total abstinence for the alcoholic? Or is it possible for a reformed alcoholic to learn to drink in moderation? With illegal drugs, the issue is somewhat different. Is it reasonable to expect a life-long heroin addict to become drug free for the rest of his life? Or should some other drug such as methadone be used in moderation as a substitute?

Professor Herbert Fingarette from the University of California at Santa Barbara, in his book *Drinking: The Myth of Alcoholism as a Disease*, questions the Alcoholics Anonymous goal of total abstinence (Fingarette, 1988). For many heavy drinkers, this cold turkey goal of no more alcohol ever is unrealistic. Instead, Fingarette says, the focus should be on teaching ways to handle stress without drinking and to develop more realistic expectations about alcohol's effects.

Psychologist G. Alan Marlatt of the University of Washington in Seattle has developed what he calls an "alcohol skills-training program," which he discusses in his book *Issues of Alcohol Use and Misuse by Young Adults* (Marlatt, 1989). The program does not promote drinking; rather, it teaches people how to drink in moderation, giving them more options and choices for safer drinking. This approach has been highly effective in drastically reducing excessive drinking among college students. Students learn how to set drinking limits and cope with peer pressure at parties and social events. In addition, students develop more realistic expectations about alcohol's mood-enhancing powers. And finally, students learn alternative methods of stress reduction or positive addictions such as running, aerobic exercise and meditation.

Similar approaches to helping adult alcoholics have been developed successfully across the United States. W. Miles Cox of the Veterans Administration Medical Center in Indianapolis and Eric Klinger of the University of Minnesota in Morris concede that a number of biological and social factors influence alcohol abuse. But they argue that final decision to drink still reflects free will. The user is still motivated by conscious or unconscious expectations that alcohol will brighten his emotional state and remove stress. Cox and Klinger have developed a technique that aims at providing alternative sources of emotional satisfaction in which the alcoholic also clarifies his major life goals and concerns. A counselor then helps the alcoholic formulate realistic weekly goals. In addition, counseling tries to reduce the tendency of the addict to use alcohol as a crutch when faced with the inevitable frustration of sometimes missing the mark (Cox, 1988, pp. 168-180).

In the final analysis, it is probably fair to say that not enough is known about which drug treatment program works best for each type of drug abuser. In other words, one size or type does not fit all, so that a multimodality approach may be necessary. Since abusers of each drug or drug type as well as different kinds of drug abusers are distinctly different, they require a variety of programs, each tailored to each drug and drug abuser, as we saw at Cafe 458 in Atlanta.

Regardless of which drug treatment program is considered best for the individual drug abuser, proponents of drug treatment would agree about three things. First, there are simply not enough openings in drug treatment programs to handle all the drug abusers who want treatment. Second, not enough financial resources are currently being allocated to drug treatment to make a serious dent in the problem of drug abuse and addiction, especially in these fiscally troubled times. Third, much more research is needed to decide which drug treatment programs are best for each type of drug abuser.

Finally, in an era when resources for drug treatment are limited, we must make sure we truly understand the nature and extent of each person's drug addiction. Those that have extreme forms of physical addiction may need medical treatment based on a disease model. But for most of the other users with moderate forms of addiction, less expensive psychological programs are probably more appropriate.

## Conclusions

Americans yearn for a quick fix to the drug abuse problem. They become frustrated when they are told that drug abuse is a condition, not a disease. Problems often have solutions, but conditions are different. The U.S. government, State and local governments are the doctors, who must work with the patient, who is the community. Together, they must manage, minimize, and reduce the severity of the condition. The government must provide the general guidance and the resources, but the condition must be worked at the community level.

While we need to put more emphasis on demand reduction, the situation will require a complex blend of demand concepts and smart supply oriented concepts (such as community policing) with a singular common denominator: time. Over time, America must accept that there will be costs and sometimes unwanted, but necessary, side effects. The old American adage, "more is better," is probably not the solution to its drug problem. As Kleiman states, "making drug policy has something in common with taking drugs: both are activities prone to excess and the key to avoiding problems with either is knowing when to stop (which sometimes means knowing when not to start)" (Kleiman, 1993).

So what will it take to manage the problem? According to Lee Brown, the recently retired Drug Czar, "Drug policy must focus on what works. It's time to end the philosophical discussion of goals and evaluations and get down to the business of identifying and funding those programs that show results . . . and dropping those that do not" (Brown, p. 28). This is an admirable objective, certainly in synchronization with the preponderance of research on alternatives and solutions to the drug problem, all calling for a non-parochial evaluation of strategy in light of diminishing resources. However, we need to exercise caution so as not to get bogged down in the minutia. The main thing is to get the priorities right.

We need to shift the amount of available dollars to support a demand reduction strategy rather than a supply reduction strategy. The Clinton FY 1996 strategy does some re-prioritization. But it's difficult to move toward more demand reduction when Democrats and Republicans in Congress are determined to move the country in the opposite direction. President Clinton must go over the heads of Congress and directly to the American people.

Admittedly, a simple changing of priorities is often easier said than done. America and its leadership must find the political will to "just do it." Recently, a senior military officer who was speaking on a different, but applicable subject, stated to his audience, "we are not likely to make tough decisions that affect the survival values of our bureaucracy." There is a lot to be said for this statement. The bureaucracy behind the supply reduction strategy is alive and well with "ricebowls" and a strong unwillingness and even contempt for making changes that would affect the growth of their organization(s). It is easier for an administration to plod along, within its political environment, demonstrating contestable results, than to courageously "belly up to the bar" and admit that the entire direction of a program, or strategy, must change – and then do it.


## Is Legalization The Answer?

Throughout the research on drug abuse, the recommendation to legalize or decriminalize all and/or selected drugs was often discussed. This was especially so when drug abuse was assessed vis-a-vis an upsurge of drug related violence. The current Clinton administration correctly does not favor legalization. Legalization is a drastic response and maybe the fail safe solution when all else has not achieved results. However, the failure flag should only be hoisted when America has truly failed, not just because the country is still groping for the right approach. There is too little evidence that suggests legalization will be the cure all for the drug problem.

Quite the contrary. The effects of alcohol legalization have had more negative repercussions in terms of deaths, accidents and health costs, etc., than any other illegal prohibitive. Experiments with drug legalization have also not been as positive as expected. Scott MacDonald points out that the legalization of drugs in the Netherlands opened a Pandora's box of problems. Quoting Mary Brady in her assessment of the impact of legalization: "For a city of 750,000 the crime file is indeed frightening. Muggings have increased sevenfold . . . 2,500 robberies, 50,000 petty theft crimes, 147 rapes, and 24 murders. The city's estimated 14,000 hard drug users are blamed for 90% of the crimes" (MacDonald, 1988, pp. 10-11). Amsterdam also attracted foreign addicts to the city. A similar problem is occurring in Zurich where, according to Roger Cohen, "addicts were drawn from all over Europe in recent years by the decision to offer clean syringes, the help of health officials, and the large measure of tolerance in the Platzspitz" (Cohen, 1993, p. 218). He continued to suggest that an experiment in tolerance and containment got out of control. In a rebuttal against a suggestion by noted economist Milton Friedman to legalize heroin, James Wilson states that, "if we changed the law to make access to cocaine and heroin easier, then the result would be a sharp increase in use, a more widespread degradation of the human personality, and a greater rate of accidents and violence" (Wilson, 1993/1994, p. 217). Finally, in searching for drug policy balance, Goldstein and Kalant state, "drug policy should strike the right balance between reducing the harm done by psychoactive drugs and reducing the harm that results from strict legal prohibitions and their enforcement. It is concluded, from a cost benefit analysis on pharmacologic, toxicologic, sociologic, and historical facts, that radical steps to repeal the prohibitions on presently illegal drugs would be likely, on balance, to make matters worse rather than better" (Goldstein, 1992/93, p. 190).

From an international perspective, Peter Smith argues against legalization. He says it would be like pulling the rug out from under the Latin American nations who have struggled with drug eradication and interdiction. "After all this promotion for drug wars, it would be politically and morally untenable to decide on unilateral legalization and thus proclaim that other countries had made their sacrifices in vain" (Smith, p. 16).

## A Message to the National Leadership

In his writings, Alvin Toffler says that using a conventional map to plan and execute policy in today's complex world is doomed to failure. America must evolve from a brute force society to a brain force society. The country needs smarter strategies (Toffler, 1993). Getting smart on drug abuse in America means that the nation must get smart on the components that affect drug abuse/use: crime, poverty, education, etc.

The Clinton administration initially selected demand reduction as the centerpiece for its national drug strategy. That was smart. At least America would have a strong foundation to build its house on. Void of agendas and constituents, the United States seriously needs to continually revamp its strategy, pruning out the deadwood, the pork barrel issues, and the trappings of interest groups. The country should accept, as an interim parallel strategy, some supply side programs such as community policing. Its demand focus should ultimately be weighted to preventing children from using drugs and changing their attitudes as well as treating the hard core addicts. Thus, the country needs to work on treatment for those hooked on drugs, but not at the expense of prevention and education. This is "damage control" for America society: some of which will succeed and some of which will fail at rehabilitation. At some point in time, the incurable will die and, if the education and prevention programs have done their job, treatment will only focus on a small portion of society that traditionally experiments with illegal substances. America must eliminate the intense desire to micromanage the drug abuse problem from the top. Through effective horizontal leadership, let the community leaders tackle this challenge.

Solving America's drug crisis should not be a Republican or Democratic ticket issue. This is a vital national interest for all Americans. The lives of America's children are at stake. As a father, the sum of my fears is a son or daughter hooked on drugs or the victim of drug related violence. The nation owes it to its children to hand America over to them in better shape than in the past. It is our generation's task to repair the structural damage caused by drug abuse so that our children may also prosper in a country that cares about all of its people.

# References

Abelin, T., et al, (1989), *Lancer*.

Bachman, J., et al, (1990), *Journal of Health and Social Behavior*.

Berger, J., (1989), *New York Times*, October 20.

Blum, K. and E. Noble, (1990), *Journal of the American Medical Association*, April.

Bohman, M. et al., (1981), Archives of General Psychiatry.

Booth, W., (1990), *Washington Post Weekly Edition*, March 26 — April 1.

Bower, B., (1988), *Science News*, August 6.

Brownson, R., (1992), *American Journal of Public Health*.

Burnam, M., (1987), *Journal of Health and Social Behavior*.

Cadoret, R., et al (1980), *Archives of General Psychiatry*.

Charen, M., (1989), *Conservative Chronicle*.

Cloninger, C. et al., (1981), Archives of General Psychiatry.

Cohen, R., (1993), in Goode, E., (ed). *Drugs, Society and Behavior*.

Cooper, M. et al., (1992), Journal of Abnormal Psychology.

Cox, W. and E. Klinger, (1988), *Journal of Abnormal Psychology*, May.

Critchlow, B., (1986) *American Psychologist*.

Diamond, J., (1987), *Whole Earth Review*, Spring.

Donovan, I. et al., (1985), *Journal of Consulting and Clinical Psychology*.

Elliott D. et al., (1989), *Multiple Problem Youth*.

Elliot, D. et al., (1982), *American Psychologist*.

Engs, R. et al., (1990), *British Journal of Addiction*.

Epstine, J., (1989), *New York Times Magazine*, July 2.

Fertig, L., (1975), *Archives of General Psychiatry*, August.

Fingarette, H., (1988), *Heavy Drinking: The Myth of Alcoholism as a Disease*.

Frank, S. et al., (1990), *Journal of Personality and Social Psychology*.

Franklyn, D., (1990), *Health*, November/December.

Glassner, W., (1976), *Positive Addiction*.

Goddard, E., (1992) *British Journal of Addiction*.

Goodwin, D. et al., (1973), *Archives of General Psychiatry*.

Goodwin, D., (1985), *Archives of General Psychiatry*.

Gottheil, E. et al., (1983), Etiologic Aspects of Alcohol and Drug Abuse.

Curling, H. et al., (1981), Twin Research.

Hamill, P. , (1988), *New York*, August 15.

Hanson, C., (1990), *Christian Science Monitor*, July 30.

Herson, H., (1977), *Journal of Studies on Alcohol*, 38.

Holden, C., (1991), *Science*, January 11.

Holloway, M., (1991), *Scientific American*, March.

Hrubeck, Z. and G. Omenn, (1981), *Alcoholism*, 1981.

Hopson, J., (1988) *Psychology Today*, July/August.

Huba, C. et al., (1979), *Journal of Consulting and Clinical Psychology*.

Huizinga, D. et al., (1991), *Urban Delinquency and Substance Abuse.*

Jessor, R. and S. Jessor, (1977), *Problem Behavior and Psychological Development.*

Johnston, L., (1987), National Trends in Drug Use and Related Factors among American High School Students and Young Adults, 1975-1986.

Jonas, G., (1990), *Saturday Night*, September.

Kandel, D., (1975), *Science.*

Kanigel, R., (1988), *Science Illustrated*, October/November.

Kilbourne, J., (1989), "Advertising Addiction," *Multinational Monitor*, June.

Kine, D., (1988), *Hippocrates*, May/June.

Kleiman, M., (1993), *Against Excess: Drug Policy for Results.*

Kozlowski, L., (1991), *British Journal of Addiction.*

Labatan, S., (1989), The Cost of Drug Abuse, *New York Times*, December 5.

Lazare, D., (1990), *The Village Voice*, January.

Lazare, D., (1989), *In These Times*, October 24.

Leigh, B., (1989), *Psychologist Bulletin.*

Levinthal, C., (1996), *Drugs, Behavior and Modern Society.*

Levison, P. et al., (1983), *Commonalities in Substance Abuse and Habitual Behaviors.*

MacDonald, S., (1988), *Dancing on a Volcano.*

Maltzman, I. and A. Schweiger, (1991), *British Journal of Addiction.*

Marlatt, G., (1988), *Issues of Alcohol Use and Misuse by Young Adults.*

Marsi, L., (1989) *Omni*, October.

McCue, M. et al., (1991), *Journal of Abnormal Psychology.*

Milan, L. and K. Ketcham, (1981), *Under the Influence.*

Nakken, C., (1988), *The Addictive Personality.*

Nathan, P. in Gotheil et. al., (1985), *Etiologic Aspects of Alcohol and Drug Abuse,*

Newsweek, (1989), *Roots of Addiction*, 20 February.

Pederson, W., (1991), *British Journal of Addiction.*

Peele, S., (1989), *The Deceasing of America.*

Peele, S., (1990), *The Atlantic,*

Peele, S. et al., (1991), *The Truth About Addiction and Recovery.*

Pekkanen, J., (1984), *The Washingtonian*, August.

Pomerleau C., (1987), *Psychology Today.*

Perry, S., (1990), *Current Health*, May.

Pickens, R. et al., (1991), *Archives of General Psychiatry.*

Rayl, A., (1989), *Omni*, December.

Robertson, N., (1988), *New York Times Magazine*, February 21.

Rose, J. and E. Levin, (1991), *British Journal of Addiction.*

Rosenthal, E., (1988), "Madison Avenue Medicine," *Discover,* October.

Schaler, J., (1991), *Society*, September/October.

Schaler, J., (1981), *Under the Influence.*

Schuckit, M., (1982), *American Journal of Psychiatry.*

Schuckit, M. et al., (1972), American Journal of Psychiatry.

Seeman, et. al., (1988).

Shedler J. and J. Block Journal of Health and Social Behavior (1990), American Psychologist.

Sheehan, G., (1978), *Running and Being.*

Sheehan, G., (1980), *This Running Life.*

Siegel, R., (1989), *Intoxication.*

Smith, P. , (1992) *Drug Policy in the Americas.*

Stein, B., (1988), *Newsday*, December 4.

Stein B. et. al., (1987), *Journal of Personalities and Social Psychology.*

Stellar, J. and E. Stellar (1985), *Neurobiology of Motivation and Reward.*

Szasz, T., (19987), *Insanity.*

Toffler, A., (1993), Lecture at Army War College, April 17.

Weil, A., (1986, *The Village Voice*, September 30.

Wheeler, C., (1987), *Insight*, February 23.

White House, (1992), *National Drug Control Strategy.*

Wilson, G., (1987), Journal of Consulting and Clinical Psychology.

Wilson, G. and D. Abrahams, (1977), *Cognitive Therapy and Research.*

Wilson, J., (1990), *Commentary*, February.

Wilson, J., (1993/4) in Goode, E. (ed.) *Drugs, Society and Behavior.*

Wise, R. and Bozrth, M, (1987), *Psychological Review.*

Wisse, R. and M. Bozarth, (1987) *Psychological Review.*

Zucker, R. and H. Fitzgerald, (1991), *Alcohol Health and Research World.*

# 7 Bibliography

## I. The Threat

Altschuler, David M. and Brounstein, Paul J., "Patterns of Drug Use, Drug Trafficking, and Other Delinquency Among Inner-city Adolescent Males in Washington, D.C.," *Criminology* (1991), 29(4):589-621.

Amaro, Hortensia; Fried, Lise E.; Cabral, Howard; and Zukeman, Barry, "Violence During Pregnancy and Substance Use," *American Journal of Public Health* (May 1990), 80(5):575-579.

Anderson, Elijah, *Streetwise: Race, Class, and Change in an Urban Community,* (Chicago: The University of Chicago Press, 1990).

Anglin, Douglas M. and Hser, Yih-Ing, "Addicted Women and Crime," *Criminology,* (1987), 25(2):359-397.

Ball, John C.; Shaffer, John W.; and Nurco, David N., "The Day-to-Day Criminality of Heroin Addicts in Baltimore–A Study in the Continuity of Offense Rates," *Drug and Alcohol Dependence* (1983), 12:119-142.

Birch and Davis Associates, Inc., *Crack Pipe as Pimp: An Eight-city Ethnographic Study of the Sex-for-Crack Phenomenon,* (Silver Spring, MD: Birch and Davis Associates Inc., April 1991).

Blumstein, Alfred; Cohen, Jacqueline; Roth, Jeffrey A.; and Visher, Christy A., eds., *Criminal Careers and Career Criminals,* Volume 1, Washington: National Academy Press, (1986).

Chaiken, Jan M. and Chaiken, Marcia R., "Drugs and Predatory Crime," in *Drugs and Crime,* Tonry, Michael and Wilson, James Q., eds., Volume 13, *Crime and Justice* (Chicago: The University of Chicago Press, 1990), 203-239.

Cleary, Joan; Burns, Alice; and Vernon, Philip, "Health care costs of medicaid methodone maintenance treatment program recipients in New York State," presented at the American Public Health Association Annual Meeting, Chicago, 1989.

Collins, James J., "Alcohol and Interpersonal Violence: Less than Meets the

Eye," in *Pathways to Criminal Violence, Weiner,* Neil Alan and Wolfgang, Marvin E., eds., (Newburg Park, CA: Sage Publications, 1989), 49-67.

Collins, James J. , ed., *Drinking and Crime: Perspectives on the Relationships Between Alcohol Consumption and Criminal Behavior* (New York: The Guilford Press, 1981).

Collins, James J.; Hubbard, Robert L.; and Rachal, J. Valley, "Expensive Drug Use and Illegal Income: A Test of Explanatory Hypotheses," *Criminology* (1985, 23(4):743-764.

Crumley, Frank E., "Substance Abuse and Adolescent Suicidal Behavior," *Journal of the American Medical Association* (1990), 263(22):3051-3056.

Dackis, Charles A., and Gold, Mark S., "Addictiveness of Central Stimulants," in *Addiction Potential of Abused Drugs and Drug Classes,* Stimmel, Barry, ed., (New York: Haworth Press, 1990), 9-26.

Deschenes, Elizabeth Piper; Anglin, Douglas M.; and Speckart, George, "Narcotics Addiction: Related Criminal Careers, Social and Economic Costs," *Journal of Drug Issues,* (Spring 1991), 21(2):383-411.

Duke, Lynne, "Flurry of Service and Promises Engulfs SE Neighborhood," *The Washington Post,* Decemberr 4, 1989, D1, D5.

Fagan, Jeffrey, "Intoxication and Aggression," in *Drugs and Crime,* Tonry, Michael, and Wilson, James Q., eds., Volume 13, *Crime and Justice,* (Chicago: The University of Chicago Press, 1990), 241-320.

Gallup Organization, *Drug Testing at Work: A Survey of American Corporations,* 1988.

Gillogley, Katherine M.; Evans, Arthur T., Hansen; Robin L.; Samuels, Steven J.; and Patra, K.K., "The Perinatal Impact of Cocaine, Amphetamine, and Opiate Use Detected by Universal Intrapartum Screening," *American Journal of Obstetrics and Gynecology* (November 1990), 163(part 1):1535-1542.

Goldstein, Paul J., "The Drugs/Violence Nexus: A Tripartite Conceptual Framework," *Journal of Drug Issues* (Fall 1985), 15(4):493-506.

Goldstein, Paul J.; Brownstein, Henry H.; Ryan, Patrick J.; and Bellucci, Patricia A.; "Crack and Homicide in New York City, 1988: A Conceptually Based Event Analysis," *Contemporary Drug Problems* (Winter 1990), 16(4):651-687.

Gomby, Deanna S. and Shiono, Patricia H., "Estimating the Number of Substance-exposed Infants," *The Future of Children* (1991), 1:17-25.

Haines, Joe D. and Sexter, Scott, "Acute Myocardial Infarction Associated with Cocaine Abuse," *Southern Medical Journal* (October 1987), 80(10):1326-1327.

Haller, Mark H., "Bootlegging: The Business and Politics of Violence" in *Violence in America,* Ted Robert Gurr, ed., (Newbury Park, CA: Sage, 1989), 146-162.

Hanzlick, Randy and Gowitt, Gerald T., "Cocaine Metabolite Detection in Homicide Victims," *Journal of the American Medical Association* (February

1991), 265(6):760-761.

Hood, Ian; Ryan, David; Monforte, Joseph; and Valentour, James, "Cocaine in Wayne County Medical Examiner's Cases," *Journal of Forensic Sciences* (May 1990), 35(3):591-600.

Hubbard, Robert L.; Marsden, Ellen Mary; Rachal, Valley J.; Harwood, Henrick J.; Cavanaugh, Elizabeth R.; and Ginzburg, M. Harold, *Drug Abuse Treatment: A National Study of Effectiveness* (Chapel Hill: University of North Carolina Press, 1989).

Huizinga David H.; Menard, Scott; and Elliott, Delbert S. "Delinquency and Drug Use: Temporal and Developmental Patterns," *Justice Quarterly* (September 1989), 6(3):419-455.

Hunt, Dana E., "Drugs and Consensual Crimes: Drug Dealing and Prostitution," in *Drugs and Crime,* Tonry, Michael and Wilson, James Q., eds. Volume 13, *Crime and Justice* (Chicago: The University of Chicago Press, 1990), 159-202.

Hurley, Robert E.; Freund, Deborah A; and Taylor, Donald E., "Emergency Room Use and Primary Care Case Management: Evidence from Four Medicaid Demonstration Programs," *American Journal of Public Health* (July 1989), 79(7):843-846.

Inciardi, James A., "Hooker, Whore, Junkie, Thief, Dealer, Doper, Cocaine Freak," in *The War on Drugs: Heroin, Cocaine, Crime, and Public Policy,* James A. Inciardi, ed., (Palo Alto, CA: Mayfield Publishing, 1986), 156-173.

Inciardi, James A., "The Impact of Drug Use on Street Crime," presented at the American Society of Criminology Annual Meeting, Washington D.C., 1981.

Inciardi, James A., "Trading Sex for Crack Among Juvenile Drug Users: A Research Note," *Contemporary Drug Problems* (Winter 1989), 16(4):689700.

Johnson, Bruce; Golstein, Paul J.; Preble, Edward; Schmeidler, Lipton; Douglas, Spunt Barry; and Miller, Thomas, *Taking Care of Business: The Economics of Crime by Heroin Abusers* (Lexington, MA: Lexington Books, 1985).

Johnson, Bruce D.; Williams, Terry; Dei, Koho A.; and Sanabria, Harry; "Drug Abuse in the Inner City: Impact on Hard-drug Users and the Community," in *Drugs and Crime,* Tonry, Michael and Wilson, James Q., eds., Volume 13, *Crime and Justice* (Chicago: The University of Chicago Press, 1990), 9-13.

Johnson, Bruce D.; Wish, Eric D.; Schmeidler, James; and Huizinga, David, "Concentration of Delinquent Offending: Serious Drug Involvement and High Delinquency Rates," *Journal of Drug Issues* (Spring 1991), 21(2):205-229.

Kerr, Peter, "Syphilis Surge with Crack Use Raises Fears on Spread of AIDS," *New York Times*, June 29, 1988, B1, B5.

Larsen, Judith, ed., "Drug Exposed Infants and Their Families: Coordinating Responses of the Legal, Medical and Child Protection System." *Executive Summary* (Washington: American Bar Association Center on Children and the Law, 1990).

Linnoila, Markku, "Psychomotor Effects of Drugs and Alcohol on Healthy
Volunteers and Psychiatric Patients," in *Advances in Pharmacology and
Therapeutics,* Vol. 8. *Drug Action Modification: Comparative Pharmacology,*
G. Olive, ed., (New York: Pergamon Press, 1979).

MacGregor, Scott N.; Keith, Louis G.; Chasnoff, Ira J.; Rosner, Marvin A.;
Chisum, Gay M.; Shaw Patricia; and Minogue, John P. , "Cocaine Use During
Pregnancy: Adverse Perinatal Outcome," *American Journal of Obstetric and
Gynecology* (September 1987), 157(3):686-690.

McBride, Duane C.; Burgman-Habermehl, Cindy; Alpert, Jeff; and
Chitwood, Dale D., "Drugs and Homicide," *Bulletin of the New York Academy
of Medicine* (June 1986), 62(5):497-508

McDermott, Joan, "High Anxiety: Fear of Crime in Secondary Schools,"
*Contemporary Education* (1980),52(1):1823.

McGlothlin, William H.; Anglin, Douglas M.; and Wilson, Bruce D.,
"Narcotic Addiction and Crime," *Criminology* (November 1978), 16(3):293-315.

Moskowitz, Herbert, "Adverse Effects of Alcohol and Other Drugs on Human
Performance." *Alcohol Health and Research World* (Summer 1985), 9(4):11-15.

"The Need for Treatment," in *Treating Drug Problems,* Gerstein, Dean R.,
and Harwood, Henrick J., eds., (Washington: National Academy Press, 1990),
58-104.

Neuspiel, D.R.; Hamel, S.C.; Hochberg, E., Greene J.; and Cambell, D.,
"Maternal Cocaine Use and Infant Behavior," *Neurotoxicology and Teratology*
(1991), 13:229-233.

Newcomb, Michael D., and Bentler, Peter M., *Consequences of Adolescent
Drug Use: Impact on the Lives of Young Adults* (Newbury Park, CA: Sage
Publications, 1988).

Norris, Michele L., "Life in P. G. Changes in the Face of Fear," *The
Washington Post,* November 6, 1989, A1.

Office of Criminal Justice Plans and Analysis, 1989 *Crime and Justice
Report for the District of Columbia,* July 1990.

Office of Criminal Justice Plans and Analysis, 1990 *Crime and Justice
Report for the District of Columbia,* June 1991.

Office of Criminal Justice Plans and Analysis, *Homicide in the District of
Columbia,* December 1988.

Office of Criminal Justice Plans and Analysis, *Homicide Report, District of
Columbia,* April 1992.

Permanen, Kai, "Alcohol and Crimes of Violence," in *The Biology of
Alcoholism, Vol. IV: Social Aspects,* Kissin, Benjamin, and Begleiter, Henri,
eds., (New York: Plenum Press, 1976), 351-444.

Phibbs, Ciaran; Bateman, David A.; and Schwartz, Racel M., "The Neonatal Costs
of Maternal Cocaine Use," *Journal of the American Medical Association*
(September 18 1991), 266(11):1521-1526.

Preble, Edward, "El Barrio Revisited," Paper Presented at the Annual

Meeting of the Society of Applied Anthropology, 1980, as reported in Paul J. Goldstein, "Drugs and Violent Crime," in *Pathways to Criminal Violence,* Neil Alan Weiner and Marvin E. Wolfgang, eds., (Newbury Park, CA: Sage, 1989), 16-48.

Reuter, Peter; MacCoun, Robert; and Murphy, Patrick, *Money from Crime: A Study of the Economics of Drug Dealing in Washington,* D.C., (Santa Monica, CA: The RAND Corporation, June 1990), vi.

Richardson, Lynda, "NW Family Holds its Ground Amid the Violence," *The Washington Post,* February 4, 1990, A1.

Roberts, Albert R., "Substance Abuse Among Men Who Batter Their Mates," *Journal of Substance Abuse Treatment,* (1988), 5:83-37.

Rohe, William M. and Burby, Raymond J., "Fear of Crime in Public Housing," *Environment and Behavior* (November 1988), 20(5):700-720.

Schuckit, Marc A., *Drug and Alcohol Abuse: A Clinical Guide to Diagnosis and Treatment, Second Edition* (New York: Plenum Press, 1984).

Shedler, Jonathan and Block, Jack, "Adolescent Drug Use and Psychological Health," *American Psychologist* (May 1990), 45(5):612-630.

Sherman, Lawrence W.; Steele, Leslie; Laufersweiler, Deborah; Hoffer, Nancy; and Julian, Sherry A., "Stray Bullets and 'Mushrooms': Random Shootings of Bystanders in Four Cities, 1977-88," *Journal of Quantitative Criminology* (1989), 5(4):300-316.

Sherman, Lawrence W., "The Drug Battle Doesn't Need Martyrs," *New York Times,* August 15, 1989.

Simpson, Dwayne, D.; Joe, George W.; Lehman, Wayne E.K.; and Sells, S.B., "Addiction Careers: Etiology, Treatment, and 12-year Follow-up Outcomes," *Journal of Drug Issues* (1986), 16(1).

Skogan, Wesley G., *Disorder and Decline: Crime and the Spiral of Decay in American Neighborhoods* (New York: The Free Press, 1990).

Skogan, Wesley G., and Maxfield, Michael G., *Coping with Crime: Individual and Neighborhood Reactions* (Beverly Hills: Sage Publications, 1981).

Skolnick, Andrew, "Illicit Drugs Take Still Another Toll: Death or Injury from Vehicle-associated Trauma," *Journal of the American Medical Association* (June 1990), 263(23):3122, 3125.

Tardiff, Kenneth, and Gross, Elliott M., "Homicide in New York City," *Bulletin of the New York Academy of Medicine* (1986), 62(5):413-426.

Taub, Richard P. ; Taylor, D. Garth; and Dunam, Jan D., *Paths of Neighborhood Change: Race and Crime in Urban America* (Chicago: The University of Chicago Press, 1984).

Wieczorek, William F.; Welte, John W.; and Abel, Ernest L., "Alcohol, Drugs and Murder: A Study of Convicted Homicide Offenders," *Journal of Criminal Justice* (1990), 18:217-227.

Wilson, James Q. and Kelling, George L., "Broken Windows," *Atlantic*

*Monthly* (March 1982), 29-38.

Wish, Eric D., "U.S. Drug Policy in the 1990s: Insights from New Data from Arrestees" *The International Journal of Addictions*, (1990-91), 25(3A):37-409.

Zahn, Margaret A., "Homicide in the Twentieth Century United States," *History and Crime: Implications for Criminal Justice Policy*, James A. Inciardi and Charles e. Faupel, eds., (Beverly Hills: Sage Publications, 1980), 111-132.

Zahn, Margaret A., and Bencivengo, Mark, "Violent Death: A Comparison Between Drug Users and Nondrug Users," *Addictive Diseases* (1974), 1:283-296.

Zuckerman, Barry; Frank, Deborah A.; Hingson, Ralph; and others, "Effects of Maternal Marijuana and Cocaine use on Fetal Growth," *New England Journal of Medicine* (March 23, 1989) 320(12):762-768.

Zwerling, Craig; Ryan, James; and Orav, Endel John, "The Efficacy of Preemployment Drug Screening for Marijuana and Cocaine in Predicting Employment Outcome," *Journal of the American Medical Association* (November 1990), 264(20):2639-2643.

## II. Patterns of Drug Use.

Anderson, William A.; Albrecht, Richard R.; McKeag, Douglas B.; Hoogh, David O.; and McGrew, Christopher A., "A National Survey of Alcohol and Drug Use by College Athletes," *The Physician and Sports Medicine* (February 1991), 19(2):91-104.

Bachman, Jerald G.; Wallace, Jr. John M.; O'Malley, Patrick M.; Johnston, Lloyd D.; Durth, Candace L.; and Neighbors, W., "Racial/Ethnic Differences in Smoking, Drinking, and Illicit Drug Use Among American High School Seniors, 1975-90," *American Journal of Public Health* (March 1991), 81(3):372-377.

Booth, William, "Crack Cocaine's Lock on Synaptic Space," *The Washington Post*, March 19, 1990, A3.

Bray, Robert M.; Marsden, Ellen L.; Guess, Lynn; Wheeless, Sara C.; Iannacchione, Vincent G.; and Keesling, Randall, *1988 Highlights: Worldwide Survey of Substance Abuse and Health Behaviors Among Military Personnel* (Research Triangle Park, NC: Research Triangle Institute, December 1988).

Burke, Kimberly Christie; Burke, Jack D.; Reigier, Darrel A.; and Rae, Donald S., "Age at Onset of Selected Mental Disorders in Five Community Populations," *Archives of General Psychiatry,* (June 1990), 47:511-518.

Fischer, Pamela J., "Estimating the Prevalence of Alcohol, Drug and Mental Health Problems in the Contemporary Homeless Population: A Review of the Literature," *Contemporary Drug Problems* (Fall 1989), 16(3):333-389.

Frances, Richard J. and Allen, Michael H., "The Interaction of Substance-use Disorders with Nonpsychotic Psychiatric Disorders," *Psychiatry*, Volume 1, Rev (Philadelphia: J.B. Lippincott Company, 1990), Chapter 42, 1-13.

Hubbard, Robert L.; Marsden, Mary Ellen; Rachal, J. Valley; Harwood,

Henrick J.; Cavanaugh, Elizabeth R.; and Ginzburg, Harold M., *Drug Abuse Treatment: A National Study of Effectiveness* (Chapel Hill: University of North Carolina Press, 1989).

Jessor, Richard and Jessor, Shirley L., *Problem Behavior and Psychosocial Development: A Longitudinal Study of Youth* (New York: Academic Press, 1977).

Kandel, Denise B., "Drug and Drinking Behavior Among Youth," in *Annual Review of Sociology*, Volume 6, Alex Inkele, Neil J. Smelser, and Ralph H. Turner, eds., 1980, 235-285.

Kandel, Denise B.; Kessler, Ronald C.; and Margulies, Rebecca C.; "Antecedents of Adolescent Initiation into Stages of Drug Use: A Developmental Analysis," *Longitudinal Research on Drug Use: Empirical Findings and Methodological Issues*, Denise B. Kandel, ed., (Washington: Hemisphere Publishing Corporation, 1978).

Kandel, Denise B. and Logan, John A., "Patterns of Drug Use from Adolescence to Young Adulthood: Periods of Risk for Initiation, Stabilization and Decline in Use," American Journal of Public Health (1984), 74(7):662.

Kleber, Herbert D., "Tracking the Cocaine Epidemic: The Drug Abuse Warning Network," *Journal of the American Medical Association* (October 23/30, 1991), 266(16):2272-2273.

McCalla, Mary Ellen and Collins, James J., "Patterns of Drug Use Among Male Arrestees in Three Urban Areas," Unpublished Paper, Research Triangle Institute, 1989.

Media General/Associated Press Poll #30, May 11-20, 1990.

Mendelson, Jack H. and Mello, Nancy K., "Commonly Abused Drugs," *Harrison's Principles of Internal Medicine*, 12th ed., Wilson, Jean D., Braunwald, Eugene, et. al., eds., (New York: McGraw-Hill Inc., 1991).

Moskowitz, Herbert, "Adverse Effects of Alcohol and other Drugs on Human Performance," *Alcohol Health and Research World*, (Summer 1985), 9(4):11-15.

Pollard, Trevor G., "Relative Addiction Potential of Major Centrally-active Drugs and Drug Classes—Inhalants and Anesthetics," *Advances in Alcohol and Substance Abuse* (1990), 9(1/2):149-165.

Resnick, Richard B.; Kestenbaum, Richard S.; and Schwartz, Lee K.; "Acute Systemic Effects of Cocaine in Man: A Controlled Study by Intranasal and Intravenous Routes," *Science*, February 1977, 195:696-698.

Robins, Lee N., "Study Childhood Predictors of Adult Antisocial Behaviour: Replications from Longitudinal Studies," *Psychological Medicine* (1978), 8:611-622.

Schuckit, Marc A., *Drug and Alcohol Abuse: A Clinical Guide to Diagnosis and Treatment*, 2nd edition, (New York: Plenum Press, 1984).

University of Michigan News and Information Services, Press Release of the Results of the Monitoring the Future Project, Ann Arbor, January 27, 1992.

## III. The Drug Business

Adler, Patricia A., *Wheeling and Dealing: An Ethnography of Upper-level Drug Dealing and Smuggling Community* (New York: Columbia University Press, 1985).

Beaty, Jonathan and Hornik, Richard, "A Torrent of Dirty Dollars," *Time*, December 18, 1989, 50-56.

Blumenthal, Ralph, *Last days of the Sicilians: At War With the Mafia, the FBI Assualt on the Pizza Connection*, (New York: Random House, Inc., 1988).

Blumstein, Alfred; Cohen, Jacqueline; Roth, Jeffrey A.; and Visher, Christy A., eds., *Criminal Careers and Career Criminals*, Volume 1 (Washington: National Academy Press, 1986).

Bagley, Bruce M., "Colombia and the War on Drugs," *Foreign Affairs*, (1988), 70-92.

Brounstein, Paul J.; Hatry, Harry P. ; Altschuler, David M.; and Blair, Louis H., *Patterns of Substance Use and Delinquency Among Inner City Adolescents* (Washington: The Urban Institute, July 1989).

Carter, David L., "Drug-related Corruption of Police Officers: A Contemporary Typology," *Journal of Criminal Justice,* 18(1990):85-98.

Collett, Merrill, *The Cocaine Connection: Drug Trafficking, and Inter-American Relations* (New York: Foreign Policy Association Headline Series, Fall 1989)

Cooper, Mary H., *The Business of Drugs* (Washington: Congressional Quarterly Inc., 1990).

Fagan, Jeffrey, "The Social Organization of Drug Use and Drug Dealing Among Urban Gangs," *Criminology*, (November 1989), 27(4):633-667.

Farah, Douglas, "Colombia's Next Leader Weighs Drug Lords' Offer," *The Washington Post*, August 5, 1990, A-26.

"Getting Banks to Just Say 'No'," *Business Week*, April 17, 1989, 16-17.

Goldstein, Paul J.; Brownstein, Henry H.; Ryan, Patrick J.; and Bellucci, Patricia, "Crack and Homicide in New York City, 1988: A Conceptually Based Event Analysis," *Contemporary Drug Problems* (Winter 1989), 16(4):651-687.

Goldstein, Paul J.; Lipton, Douglas S.; Preble, Edward; Sobel, Ira; Miller, Tom; Abbott, William; Paige, William; and Soto, Franklin, "The Marketing of Street Heroin in New York City," *Journal of Drug Issues* (Summer 1984), 553-566.

Horwitz, Sari, "Violent Gangs 'All Over City,' D.C. Chief says," *The Washington Post*, September 21, 1991, A1, A8.

Henderson, Gary L., "Designer Drugs: Past History and Future Prospects," *Journal of Forensic Sciences* (March 1988),33(2):569-575.

"Heroin-based 'Designer' Drug Kills 11 in Three Northeast States," *The Washington Post,* February 4, 1991, A12.

Hibbs, Jonathan; Perper, Joshua; and Winek, Charles L., "An Outbreak of

Designer Drug-related Deaths in Pennsylvania," *Journal of the American Medical Association* (1991), 265(8):1011-1013.

Johnson, Bruce D.; Goldstein, Paul J.; Preble, Edward; Schmeidler, James; Lipton, Douglas S.; Spunt, Barry; and Miller, Thomas, *Taking Care of Business: The Economics of Crime by Heroin Abusers* (Lexington, MA: Lexington Books, 1985).

Johnson, Bruce D.; Williams, Terry; Dei, Kojo A.; Sanabria, Harry; "Drug Abuse in the Inner City: Impact on Hard-drug Users and the Community," *Drugs and Crime*, Volume 13, Crime and Justice, Michael Tonry and James Q. Wilson, eds., (Chicago: The University of Chicago Press, 1990).

"Just Dying for a Fix," *Time*, February 18, 1991, 45.

Karchmer, Clifford, *Illegal Money Laundering: A Strategy and Resource Guide for Law Enforcement Agencies* (Washington: Police Executive Research Forum, April 1988).

Karchmer, Clifford L., *Strategies for Combatting Narcotics Wholesalers*, (Washington: Police Executive Research Forum, forthcoming).

Kleiman, Mark A.R., *Marijuana: Cost of Abuse, Cost of Control* (New York: Greenwood Press, 1989).

Klein, Malcolm W., Maxson, Cheryl L. and Cunnigham, Lea C.," 'Crack,' Street Gangs, and Violence," *Criminology* (1991)

Langone, Anthony V., "IRS Criminal Investigation Tackles Money Laundering," *The Police Chief* (January 1988), 5(1):52-54.

Mahar, Maggie, "Dirty Money: It Triggers a Bold, New Attack in the War on Drugs," *Barron's*, June 26, 1989, 69(26):6-38.

Manning, Carl, "Army Rescues Hostages, but 12 Judges Reported Dead in Ministry Siege," *The Associated Press*, November 8, 1985.

Mieczkowski, "Crack Distribution in Detroit." Paper presented at the American Society of Criminology Annual Meeting, Chicago, 1988.

Mieczkowski, Thomas, "Geeking Up and Throwing Down: Heroin Street Life in Detroit," *Criminology* (1986), 24(4):645-666.

Miller, Norman S.; Gold, Mark S.; and Millman, Robert B. "Cocaine: General Characteristics, Abuse, and Addiction," *New York State Journal of Medicine* (July 1989),89(7):390-395.

Moore, Mark H., "Limiting Supplies of Drugs to Illicit Markets," *Journal of Drug Issues* (Spring 1979), 9:291-308.

Moore, Mark H., "Policies to Achieve Discrimination on the Effective Price of Heroin," *American Economic Review* (May 1973)63(2):270-277.

Murphy, Sheigla and Waldorf, Dan, "Kickin' Down to the Street Doc: Shooting Galleries in the San Francisco Bay Area," *Contemporary Drug Problems* (Spring 1991), 18(1):9-29.

Nadelmann, "Unlaundering Dirty Money Abroad: U.S. Foreign Policy and Financial Secrecy Jurisdictions," *Inter-American Law Review* (1986), 18(1):33-81.

Pharmaceutical Manufacturers Association, Facts at a Glance, Washington (1989).

Pharmaceutical Manufacturers Association, Modern Medicines: Saving lives and Money, Washington (1989).

"Potent Heroin Hitting Streets of Baltimore," Narcotics Control Digest (October 9, 1991), 21(21):6.

Puder, Karoline S.; Kagan, Doreen V.; and Morgan, John P. ; "Illicit Methamphetamine: Analysis, Synthesis, and Availability," American Journal of Drug and Alcohol Abuse (1988), 14(4):463-473.

Reuter, Peter, Disorganized Crime: The Economics of the Visible Hand (Cambridge, MA: MIT Press, 1983),

Reuter, Peter, "Eternal Hope: America's Quest for Narcotic Control," The Public Interest (Spring 1985), 79:79-95.

Reuter, Peter and Haaga, John, The Organization of High-level Drug Markets: An Exploratory Study (Santa Monica, CA: The RAND Corporation, February 1989), RAND/N-2830-NIJ.

Reuter, Peter and Kleiman, Mark A.R., "Risks and Prices: An Economic Analysis of Drug Enforcement," Crime and Justice, Michael Tonry and Norval Morris, eds., Volume 7 (Chicago: The University of Chicago Press, 1986), 289-340.

Reuter, Peter; MacCoun, Robert; and Murphy, Patrick, Money From Crime: A Study of the Economics of Drug Dealing in Washington, D.C. (Santa Monica, CA: The RAND Corporation, June, 1990), RAND/R-3894-RF.

Sen, Sankar, "Drug War in Colombia," Police Journal (April 1990), 63(2):153-158.

Smith, Clayton L., "The Controlled Substance Analogue Enforcement Act of 1986: The Compromising of Criminalization," American Journal of Criminal Law (1988),16(1):107-138.

Pergel, Irving A. , "Youth Gangs: Continuity and Change," Crime and Justice: A Review of Research, Michael Tonry and Norval Morris, eds., Volume 12 (Chicago: The University of Chicago Press, 1990), 171-275.

The Financial Action Task Force on Money Laundering Report, 1990-1991 (Paris: May 13, 1991. ).

"The Pothouse Effect," The Economist (December 15, 1990), 24.

Treaster, Joseph B., "Colombia Judges and Their Aides go on Strike to Demand Protection," New York Times, November 4, 1989,4.

Verebey, Karl and Gol, Mark S. "From Cocoa Leaves to Crack: The Effects of Dose and Routes of Administration in Abuse Liability," Psychiatric Annals, (September 1988), 18(9) : 513 -520.

Villa, John K., Banking Crimes (New York: Clark Boardman Co. Ltd., 1988).

White, Peter T., "The Poppy," National Geographic, February 1985, 167(2):142-189.

Williams, *The Cocaine Kids: The Inside Story of a Teenage Drug Ring* (Reading MA: Addison-Wesley, 1989).

Zeese, Kevin B. , "Drug-related Corruption of Public Officials," *Drug Law Report* (March-April 1986), 1 (20) : 229-237.

Zucchino, David; Rosenberg, Amy; and Gibbons, Jr., Thomas J., "U.S. Probes Drug Deaths in Region," *Philadelphia Inquirer*, March 8, 1991,1.

## IV. History of Drug Control

Bray, Robert M.; Marsden, Mary Ellen; Guess, Lynn; Wheeless, Sara C.; Iannacchione, Vincent G.; and Keesling, Randall S., *1988 Worldwide Survey of Substance Abuse and Health Behaviors Among Military Personnel* (Research Triangle Park,NC : Research Triangle Institute, 1988).

Haaga, John G., and Reuter, Peter, *The Limits of the Czar's Ukase: Drug Policy at the Local Level* (Santa Monica: The RAND Corporation, June 1990),

Inciardi, James A., *The War on Drugs: Heroin, Cocaine, Crime, and Public Policy* (Palo Alto, CA: Mayfield Publishing Company, 1986).

Kleiman, Mark A.R., and Smith, Kerry D., "State and Local Drug Enforcement: In Search of a Strategy," *Drugs and Crime*, Michael, Tonry and James Q. Wilson, eds., Volume 13, *Crime and Justice* (Chicago: The University of Chicago Press, 1990) 69-108.

Lauderdale, Pat and Inverarity, James, "Regulation of Opiates," *Journal of Drug Issues* (1984), 3: 567-577.

Morgan, Wayne H., *Drugs in America* (Syracuse University Press, 1981).

Musto, David F. *The American Disease: Origins of Narcotic Control* (New York: Oxford University Press, 1987).

Musto, David F. , "America' s First Cocaine Epidemic," *Wilson Quarterly* (Summer 1989, 13(3):59-64.

The National Association of Attorneys General and the National District Attorneys Association, Executive Working Group for Federal-State-Local Prosecutorial Relations, "Toward a Drug-free America: Nationwide Blueprint for State and Local Drug Control Strategies," December 1988.

Oakes, Richard T., "Marijuana and Economic Due Process: A Transition From Prohibition to Regulation," *Contemporary Drug Problems* (Winter 1980), 401-435.

Peyrot, Mark, "Cycles of Social Problem Development: The Case of Drug Abuse," *The Sociological Quarterly*, (1984), 25(1): 83-96.

Wilson, James Q., "Drugs and Crime," *Drugs and Crime*, Michael Tonry and James Q. Wilson, eds., Volume 13, *Crime and Justice* (Chicago: The University of Chicago Press, 1990), 521-545.

## V. Public Opinion on Drugs

ABC News Polling Unit, 1986.

Bachman, Jerald G.; Johnston, Lloyd D.; and O'Malley, Patrick, "Explaining the Recent Decline in Cocaine Use Among Young Adults: Further Evidence That Perceived Risks and Disapproval Lead to Reduced Drug Use" *Journal of Health and Social Behavior* (1990), 31:173-184.

Colasanto, Diane, "Widespread Public Opposition to Drug Legalization," *The Gallup Poll Monthly* (Princeton, NJ: The Gallup Poll, January 1990), 292: 2-8.

Elam, Stanley M., "The 22nd Annual Gallup Poll of the Public's Attitudes Toward the Public Schools," *Phi Delta Kappan* (September 1990), 72 (1): 41-55.

Elam, Stanley M.; Rose, Lowell C.; and Gallu, Alec M., "The 23rd Annual Gallup Poll of the Public's Attitudes Toward the Public Schools," *Phi Delta Kappan* (September 1991), 73 (1): 41-56.

*The Gallup Organization for the Institute for a Drug-free Workplace,* December 1989.

*The Gallup Poll Monthly* (Princeton, NJ: The Gallup Poll, May 1991), 308. "The Gallup Report," (Princeton, NJ: The Gallup Poll, September 1988), 276 : 31.

The Gallup Report (Princeton, NJ: The Gallup Poll, June 1989), 285.

General Social Survey Trend Data, 1984 to 1990, unpublished data.

Harris, Louis, *The Harris Poll* (Los Angeles: Creators Sydicate, Inc. (August 27, 1989).

Kagay, Michael R., "As Candidates Hunt the Big Issue, Polls Can Give Them a Few Clues," *New York Times*, October 20, 1991, 3.

Media General/*Associated Press Poll #30*, May 11-20, 1990.

NFO Research, Inc., *Final Report, Drug Awareness and Attitude Study* (Chicago: NFO Research, Inc., 1990).

The National Opinion Research Center, The Roper Public Opinion Research Center.

*New York Times*/CBS News Poll, 1986.

Shoemaker, Pamela J.; Wanta, Wayne; and Leggett, Dawn, "Drug Coverage and Public Opinion, 1972-1986," in *Communication Campaigns About Drugs: Government, Media, and the Public*, Pamela J. Shoemaker, ed., (Hillsdale, NJ: Lawrence Erlbaum Associates, Publishers, 1989), 67-80.

The Sixth Annual Hearst Survey, "The American Public's Hopes and Fears for the Decade of the 1990s: A National Survey of Public Awareness and Personal Opinion," (New York: The Hearst Corporation, 1989).

Skzycki, Cindy, "Poll Finds Backing for Drug Tests: One-quarter Report Abuse in Workplace," *The Washington Post*, December 14, 1989, D1 and E10.

"Surveys of the Attitudes of American Adults and Teenagers Towards the Drug Crisis and Drug Policy," *Press Release* (Princeton, NJ: The George H. Gallup International Foundation, August 4, 1989).

## VI. Drug Laws, Policies and Programs

*A Guide to State Controlled Substances Acts* (Washington: National Criminal Justice Association, January 1991),

*Alcoholics Anonymous: The Story of How Many Thousands of Men and Women Have Recovered From Alcoholism* (New York: Alcoholics Anonymous World Services, Inc., 1976).

The American Medical Association, *Home Medical Encyclopedia: Volume 2,1-Z,* (New York: Random House, 1989).

Anglin, M. Douglas and Yih-Ing Hser, "Treatment of Drug Abuse," *Drugs and Crime*, Michael Tonry and James Q. Wilson, eds., Volume 13, *Crime and Justice* (Chicago: The University of Chicago Press, 1990), 393-460.

Batten, Helen, Brandeis University, Paper Presented at the American Public Health Association Annual Meeting, Atlanta, Georgia, November 1991.

Botvin, Gilbert J., "Substance Abuse Prevention: Theory, Practice, and Effectiveness," in *Drugs and Crime,* Michael Tonry and Wilson, James Q., eds., Volume 13, *Crime and Justice* (Chicago: The University of Chicago Press, 1990), 461-512.

Bray, Robert M. , Marsden, Mary Ellen; Herbol, John R.; and Peterson, Michael R., "Progress Toward Eliminating Drug and Alcohol Abuse Among U. S. Military Personnel" *Armed Forces and Society*, July 1991.

Chaiken, Jan M.; and Chaiken, Marcia R.; "Drugs and Predatory Crime," *Drugs and Crime*, Michael Tonry and James Q. Wilson, eds., Volume 13, *Crime and Justice* (Chicago: The University of Chicago Press, 1990), 203-239.

"Drug Abuse Prevention Strategies: Board of Trustees Report," *Journal of the American Medical Association* (April 24, 1991), 265 (16): 2102-2107.

Foundation for Health Services Research, "New Data Available From 1990 Drug Services Research Survey," *Connection* (June 1992), 1 (2): 4-5.

Gilbert, Francis S., "Development of a 'Steps Questionnaire,' " *Journal of Studies on Alcohol* (1991), 52(4):353-360.

Hubbard, Robert L.; Marsden, Mary Ellen; Rachal, J. Valley; Harwood, Henrick J.; Cavanaugh, Elizabeth R.; and Ginzburg, Harold M., *Drug Abuse Treatment: A National Study of Effectiveness* (Chapel Hill: University of North Carolina Press, 1989).

Jellinek, Paul S. and Hearri, Ruby P. , "Fighting Drug Abuse at the Local Level," *Issues in Science and Technology* (Summer 1991), 7(4): 78-84.

Nace, Edgar P. , "Alcoholics Anonymous," *Substance Abuse: A Comprehensive Textbook,* Joyce H. Lowinson, Pedro Ruiz, and Robert B. Millman, eds., (Baltimore: Williams & Wilkins 1992), 486-495.

*Narcotics Anonymous*, 5th Edition (Van Nuys, CA: World Service Office, Inc. , 1988).

Renz, Loren, *Alcohol & Drug Abuse Funding: An Analysis of Foundation Grants,* The Foundation Center, 1989.

Rosenbaum, Dennis; Ringwalt, Chris; Curtin, Thomas R.; Wilkinson, Deanna; Davis, Brenda; and Taranowski, Chet, *A Second Year Evaluation of DARE in Illinois* (Springfield, IL: Illinois State Police, 1991).

*State Resources and Services Related to Alcohol and Other Drug Abuse Problems for Fiscal Year 1990* (Washington: National Association of State Alcohol and Drug Abuse Directors, November 1991).

Constance Thomas, *1990 State Substance Abuse Laws, Intergovernmental Health Policy Project,* (Washington: George Washington University, March 1991).

Thorne, Judy M.; Holley, Judy A.; Wine, Jennifer; Hayward, Becky J.; and Ringwalt, Christopher L., *A Study of the Drug-Free Schools and Communities Act: Report on State and Local Programs,* U.S. Department of Education Contract LC8802801 (Research Triangle Park, NC: Research Triangle Institute, 1991).

United Nations, *Report of the International Narcotics Control Board for 1990,* New York, 1990.

Villa, John K., *Banking Crimes: Fraud, Money Laundering and Embezzlement* (New York: Clark Boardman, Co., Ltd., 1988).

Wodraska, Dorothy, "Project 1-Star," *Juvenile Justice Digest* (August 21, 1991), 19(16): 2-4.

## VII. Drug Testing

AMA, Council on Scientific Affairs, "Scientific Issues in Drug Testing," *Journal of the American Medical Association* (1987), 257 (22): 3110-3114.

American Correctional Association, *Drug Abuse Testing: Successful Models for Treatment and Control in Correctional Programs,* Second Edition, 1981.

The APT Foundation Task Force, *Report on Drug and Alcohol Testing in the Workplace,* (New Haven, CT: The APT Foundation, 1988).

Bailey, David N., "Drug Screening in an Unconventional Matrix: Hair Analysis" (editorial), *Journal of the American Medical Association* (1989), 262(23): 3331.

Beckwith, Raana; McClelland, Ann; and Geiger, Walton, "Instant Kokowski," *Proceedings of the Fifth National Conference on Methadone Treatment,* 2(1973): 1060-1063.

Bray, Robert M.; Marsden, Mary Ellen; Guess, L. Lynn; Wheeless, Sara C.; Lannacchione, Vincent G.; and Keesling, S. Randall, *Highlights 1988 Worldwide Survey of Substance Abuse and Health Behaviors Among Military Personnel* (Research Triangle Park, NC: Research Triangle Institute, 1990).

Cochin, J. and Daly, J.W., "Rapid Identification of Analgesic Drugs in Urine with Thin-layer Chromatography," *Experientia* (1962), 18: 294-295.

Delogu, Nancy N., "ACLU Targets State Legislatures," *The Drug Free Workplace Report* (1991), III(1): 13.

Dole, Vincent P. ; Kim, Wan Kyun; and Eglitis, Ilze, "Detection of Narcotic Drugs, Tranquilizers, Amphetamines, and Barbiturates in Urine," *Journal of the American Medical Association* (1966), 198(4): 115-118.

Dole, Vincent P. , and Nyswander, Marie, "A Medical Treatment for Diacetylmorphone (heroin) Addiction," *Journal of the American Medical Association* (1965), 193(8): 80-84.

Gallup Organization, *Drug Testing at Work: A Survey of American Corporations, 1988.*

Geiger, Walton, "Cocaine — with Speed," *Proceedings of the Fifth National Conference on Methadone Treatment*, 2(1973): 1064-1065.

Jaffe, Jerome H., "Footnotes in the Evolution of the American National Response: Some Little Known Aspects of the First American Strategy for Drug Abuse and Drug Traffic Prevention." The Inaugural Thomas Okey Memorial Lecture, *British Journal of Addiction* (1987), 82:587-600.

Kokowski, Robert J.; Hamner, Samuel; and Shiplet, Myron, "Detection of the Use of Methaqualone and Benzodiazepines in Urine Screening Programs," *Proceedings of the Fifth National Conference on Methadone Treatment,* 2(1973): 1073-1078.

Marshall, Eliot, "Testing Urine for Drugs" *Science* (1988), 241(4862): 150-152.

Musto, David F., *The American Disease: Origins of Narcotics Control* (New York: Oxford University Press, 1987).

Robins, Lee N.; Davis, Darlene H.; and Nurco, David N.; "How Permanent was Vietnam Drug Addiction?" *American Journal of Public Health Supplement* (1974), 64: 38-43.

Rosen, Cathryn Jo and Goldkamp, John S., "The Constitutionality of Drug Testing at the Bail Stage," *Journal of Criminal Law & Criminology* (1989), 80(I): 114-176.

Sokolowski, James M., "Government Drug Testing: A Question of Reasonableness," *Vanderbilt Law Review* (May 1990), 43(4): 1343-1376.

Spector, Sydney and Parker, Charles W., "Morphine: Radioimmunoassay," *Science* (June 1970),168 (3937): 1347-1348.

Thomas, Constance, *1990 State Substance Abuse Laws, Intergovernmental Health Policy Project,* (Washington: George Washington University, March 1991).

Wish, Eric D. and Gropper, Bernard A., "Drug Testing by the Criminal Justice System: Methods, Research, and Applications," in *Drugs and Crime,* Tonry, Michael and Wilson, James Q., eds., (Chicago: University of Chicago Press, 1990), 321-391.

## VIII. Costs of Drug Use and Control

Bersharov, Douglas J., "The Children of Crack: Will We Protect Them?" *Public Welfare* (Fall 1989), 6-11,42.

Cowan, Terrence R., "Drugs and the Workplace: To Drug Test or Not to Test?" *Public Personnel Management* (Winter 1987), 16(4): 313-322.

Goerdt, John; Lomvardias, Chris; Gallaw, Geoff; and Mahoney, Barry, *Examining Court Delay: The Pace of Litigation in 26 Urban Trial Courts, 1987,* (Williamsburg, VA: National Center of State Courts, 1989).

Gomby, Deanna and Shiono, Patricia H., "Estimating the Number of Substance-exposed Infants," *The Future of Children,* (Spring 1991), 1: I 7- 25.

Krizay, John, *The Fifty Billion Dollar Drain* (Irvine, CA: Care Institute, 1986). Phibbs, Ciaran S., Bateman, David A., and Schwartz, Rachel M., The Neonatal Costs of Maternal Cocaine Use," *Journal of the American Medical Association* (September 18, 1991), 266(11): 1521-1526.

*State Court Caseload Statistics: Annual Report 1988* (Williamsburg, VA: National Center for State Courts, February 1990).

Zwerling, Craig; Ryan, James; and Orav, Endel John, "The Efficacy of Preemployment Drug Screening for Marijuana and Cocaine in Predicting Employment Outcome," *Journal of the American Medical Association* (November 28, 1990), 264(20): 2639-2643.

## IX. Drug Law Enforcement

*A Guide to State Controlled Substances Acts* (Washington: National Criminal Justice Association, January 1991).

Abadinsky, Howard, *Drug Abuse: An Introduction* (Chicago: Nelson-Hall, Inc., 1989).

Barr, Robert and Pease, Ken, "Crime Placement, Displacement, and Deflection," *Crime and Justice: A Reveiw of Research,* Tonry, Michael and Morris, Norval, eds., Volume 12, *Crime and Justice* (Chicago: The University of Chicago Press, 1989), 277-318.

Bocklet, Richard, "National Guard Drug Mission Help to Law Enforcement," *Law and Order* (June 1990), 38(6): 71-77.

Conner, Roger and Burns, Patrick, *The Winnable War: A Community Guide to Eradicating Street Drug Markets* (Washington: American Alliance for Rights & Responsibilities, 1991).

Cushing, Michael A., "Combatting Street Level Narcotics," *Police Chief* (October 1989), LVI(10): 113-116.

Eck, John E., *Police and Drug Control: A Home Field Advantage* (Washington: Police Executive Research Forum, 1989).

*The Financial Action Task Force on Money Laundering Report,* 1990-1991

(Paris: May 13, 1991).

Gates, Daryl F., "Project DARE — A Challenge to Arm our Youth," *The Police Chief* (October 1987), 50(10): 100-101.

Gerth, Jeff, "Bank's $15 Million Penalty for Laundering is Largest Ever," *New York Times,* February 6, 1990, D24.

"Getting the Banks to Just Say 'No'," *Business Week,* April 17, 1989, 16-17.

Isikoff, Michael, "CIA Creates Narcotics Unit to Help in Drug Fight," *The Washington Post,* May 28,1989, A12-A 13.

Karchmer, Clifford L., *Illegal Money Laundering: A Strategy and Resource Guide for Law Enforcement Agencies* (Washington: Police Executive Research Forum, April 1988).

Karchmer, Clifford L., "Money Laundering and the Organized Underworld," *Politics and Economics of Organized Crime,* Alexander, Herbert E. and Caiden, Gerald E., eds., (Lexington, MA: Lexington Books, 1985), 37-48.

Kleiman, Mark, "Organized Crime and Drug Abuse Control," in *Major Issues in Organized Crime Control,* Edelhurtz, Herbert, ed., (Bellevue, WA: Northeast Policy Studies Center, 1987).

Kleiman, Mark and Smith, Kerry D., "State and Local Drug Enforcement: In Search of a Strategy," *Drugs and Crime,* Tonry, Michael and Wilson, James Q., eds., Volume 13, *Crime and Justice* (Chicago: The University of Chicago Press, 1990), 69-108.

Laszlo, Anna T., "Clandestine Drug Laboratories: Confronting a Growing National Crisis," *The National Sheriff* (August-September 1989), 9-14.

Mahar, Maggie, "Dirty Money: It Triggers a Bold, New Attack in the War on Drugs," *Barron's,* June 26, 1989, 6-38.

Martens, Frederick T., "Narcotics Enforcement: What are the Goals and Do They Conflict?" Villanova University, Organized Crime Narcotics Enforcement Symposium, May 1988.

Marx, Gary T., *Undercover: Police Surveillance in America,* A Twentieth Century Fund Book, (Berkeley, CA: University of California Press, 1988).

Moore, Mark H., "Supply Reduction and Drug Law Enforcement," *Drugs and Crime,* Tonry, Michael and Wilson, James Q., eds., Volume 13, *Crime and Justice* (Chicago: The University of Chicago Press, 1990), 109-157.

Moore, Mark H., *Buy and Bust: The Effective Regulation of an Illicit Market in Heroin* (Lexington, MA: Lexington Books, 1977).

Nadelmann, Ethan, "Unlaundering Dirty Money Abroad: U.S. Foreign Policy and Financial Secrecy Jurisdictions," *Inter-American Law Review* (1986), 18(1): 33-81.

National League of Cities, *Front Line Reports: Local Strategies in the War Against Drugs,* November 1989.

Reuter, Peter, "Eternal Hope: America's Quest for Narcotics Control," *Public Interest* (Spring 1985), 79: 79-95.

Reuter, Peter; Haaga, John; Murphy, Patrick; and Praskac, Amy, *Drug Use and Drug Programs in the Washington Metropolitan Area* (Santa Monica: The RAND Corporation, 1988).

Stewart, David O., "The Drug Exception," *ABA Journal* (May 1990), 42-48.

Trojanowicz, Robert and Bucqueroux, Bonnie, *Community Policing: A Contemporary Perspective* (Cincinnati: Anderson Publishing Co., 1990).

Villa, John K., *Banking Crimes: Fraud, Money Laundering, and Embezzlement* (New York: Clark Boardman Co., Ltd., 1988).

Weisel, Deborah Lamm, "Playing the Home Field: A Problem-oriented Approach to Drug Control," *American Journal of Police* (1990), 9(1): 75-95.

Weisel, Deborah Lamm, *Tackling Drug Problems in Public Housing: A Guide for Police* (Washington: Police Executive Research Forum, 1990)

Zimmer, Lynn, "Proactive Policing Against Street-level Drug Trafficking," *American Journal of Police* (1990), 9(1): 43-74.

## X. Drug Prosecution and Adjudication

Abadinsky, Howard, *Drug Abuse: An Introduction* (Chicago: Nelson-Hall Inc., 1989).

Belenko, Steven, "The Impact of Drug Offenders on the Criminal Justice System," *Drugs, Crime and the Criminal Justice System*, Ralph Weisheit, ed., (Cincinnati: Anderson Publishing Co. and the Academy of Criminal Justice Sciences, 1990), 27-78.

Goerdt, John; Lomvardias, Chris; Gallas, Geoff; and Mahoney, B., *Examining Court Delay: The Pace of Litigation in 26 Urban Trial Courts, 1987* (Williamsburg, VA: National Center for State Courts, 1989).

Goerdt, John A. and Martin, John A. "The Impact of Drug Cases on Case Processing in Urban Trial Courts," *State Court Journal* (Fall 1989), 13(4): 4-12.

Henderson, Thomas A., "Judicial Management Strategies for Addressing Drug Caseload," A Paper Presented to *Managing Drug-related Cases in Urban Trial Courts*, National Center for State Courts, July 17-18, 1989.

Lipscher, Robert D., "The Judicial Response to the Drug Crisis," *State Court Journal* (Fall 1989), 13(4): 13-17.

Lyman, Michael D., *Practical Drug Enforcement: Procedures and Administration* (New York: Elsevier Science Publishing Co., Inc., 1989).

Marcus, Ruth, "Panel Advises Changes in Hearing Drug Cases," *The Washington Post,* April 3, 1990, A17.

Rosen, Cathryn Jo and Goldkamp, John S., "The Constitutionality of Drug Testing at the Bail Stage," *The Journal of Criminal Law and Criminology* (1989), 80(1): 114-176.

Schneider, Anne L., "A Comparative Analysis of Juvenile Court Responses to Drug and Alcohol Offenses," *Crime and Delinquency* (January 1988), 34(1):

103-124.

Sickmund, Melissa, *Juvenile Court Drug and Alcohol Cases*, 1985-88, (Pittsburgh: National Center for Juvenile Justice, September 1990).

Smith, Douglas A. Wish, Eric D., and Jarjoura, G. Roger, "Drug Use and Pretrial Misconduct in New York City," *Journal of Quantitative Criminology* (1989), 5(2): 101-126.

Visher, Christy A., and Linster, Richard L., "A Survival Model of Pretrial Failure," *Journal of Quantitative Criminology* (1990), 6(2): 153-184.

## XI. Sentencing and Sanctions

*A Guide to State Controlled Substances Acts* (Washington: National Criminal Justice Association, January 1991).

Crowe, Ann H., *Drug Testing in the Juvenile Justice System: The Necessary Correlation Between Agency Mission, Program Purpose and Use of Test Results*, American Probation and Parole Association.

"Drug Lord Sentenced to Death," *USA Today*, May 15, 1991, 3a.

"Jury Recommends Execution Under New U.S. Drug Law," *The Washington Post*, April 4, 1991, A 10.

McCarthy, Belinda R., ed., *Intermediate Punishments: Intensive Supervision, Home Confinement, and Electronic Surveillance* (Monsey, N.Y.: Criminal Justice Press, 1987).

*National Narcotics Intervention Project*, American Probation and Parole Association/National Association of Probation Executives, unpublished data.

*Preliminary Report on the Development and Impact of the Minnesota Sentencing Guidelines,* Minnesota Sentencing Guidelines Commission, July 1982.

Sickmund, Melissa, *Juvenile Court Drug and Alcohol Cases,* 1985-88, (Pittsburgh: National Center for Juvenile Justice, September 1990).

Scotkin, Ronnie M., "The Development of the Federal Sentencing Guidelines for Drug Trafficking Offenses," *Criminal Law Bulletin* (January/February 1990), 26:50-59.

Texas Comptroller of Public Accounts, Economic Analysis Center, "Texas Drug Tax Sets New Trap for Drug Dealers," *Fiscal Notes,* October 1989, 6-7.

Thomas, Constance, *1990 State Substance Abuse Laws*, Intergovernmental Health Policy Project (Washington: George Washington University, March 1991).

Thompson, Tracy, "Electronically Monitored House Arrest Far From Perfect," *The Washington Post*, December 10, 1990, D1.

Vaughn, Joseph B., "A Survey of Juvenile Electronic Monitoring and Home Confinement Programs," *Juvenile & Family Court Journal* (1989), 1-36.

Villa, John K., *Banking Crimes: Fraud, Money Laundering, and*

*Embezzlement* (New York: Clark Boardman, Co., Ltd., 1988).

Wilson, Deborah G., "The Impact of Federal Sentencing Guidelines on Community Corrections and Privatization," *The U.S. Sentencing Guidelines: Implications for Criminal Justice,* Champion, Dean J., ed., (New York: Praeger, 1989).

## XII. Correctional Populations

*A Guide to State Controlled Substances Acts* (Washington: National Criminal Justice Association, 1991).

Babst, Dean V., *Drug Abuse Testing: Successful Models For Treatment And Control in Correctional Programs, 2nd Edition* (College Park, MD: American Correctional Association, July 1981).

Camp, George M. and Camp, Camille Graham, *The Corrections Yearbook, 1991: Adult Corrections* (South Salem, NY: Criminal Justice Institute, 1991).

Camp, George M. and Camp, Camille Graham, *The Corrections Yearbook 1991: Probation and Parole* (South Salem, NY: Criminal Justice Institute, 1991).

Camp, George M. and Camp, Camille Graham, *The Corrections Yearbook, 1991: Juvenile Corrections* (Sourth Salem, NY: Criminal Justice Institute, 1991).

Clayton, Richard R., Walden, Katherine P. , and Bennett, Gary T., *Surveillance and Treatment on Probation (STOP) in Kentucky: An Evaluation,* Revised Summary (Lexington, KY: Center for Prevention Research, June 1990).

Collins, James J., "Policy Choices in Urine Testing of Probationers and Parolees," Paper Presented at the American Society of Criminology, Annual Meeting in Reno, Nevada, November 1989.

Collins, James J. and Allison, Margaret, "Legal Coercion and Retention in Drug Abuse Treatment," *Hospital and Community Psychiatry* (1983), 34(12): 1145-1149.

Collins, James J.; Hubbard, Robert J.; Rachal, J. Valley; Cavanaugh, Elizabeth R.; and Craddock, S. Gail, *Criminal Justice Clients in Drug Treatment* (Research Triangel Park, NC: Research Triangle Institute, 1982).

Eisenberg, Michael, *Factors Associated with Recidivism* (Austin, TX: Texas Board of Pardons and Paroles, 1985).

Gallagher, Jerome J. and Manary, Joseph C., *Treatment of the Heroin Addict: A Correction-rehabilitation Model* (Mason, MI: Ingham County Jail, no date).

Gerstein, Dean R. and Harwood, Henrick J., eds., *Treating Drug Problems,* Volume 1 (Washington: National Academy Press, 1990).

Hubbard, Robert L.; Marsden, Mary Ellen; Rachal, J. Valley; Harwood, Henrick J.; Cavanaugh, Elizabeth R.; and Ginzburg, Harold M., *Drug Abuse Treatment: A National Study of Effectiveness,* (Chapel Hill, NC: University of

North Carolina Press, 1989).

"Interview with American Jail Association (AJA) Special Projects Director," *American Jails* (Fall 1988), 54-56.

Klein, Stephen P. and Caggiano, Michael N., *The Prevalence, Predictability, and Policy Implications of Recidivism* (Santa Monica: The RAND Corporation, 1986).

Leukefeld, Carl G, "Opportunities for Strengthening Community Corrections with Coerced Drug Abuse Treatment," *Perspectives,* Fall 1990, 6-9.

Marlette, Marjorie, "Drug Treatment Programs for Inmates," *Corrections Compendium* (August 1990), 15(6).

Matthews, Timothy H., "The National Narcotics Intervention Training Program: Say Yes to Drug Intervention," *Perspectives* (Summer 1988), 12(3): 16-27.

Petersilia, Joan; Peterson, Joyce; and Turner, Susan, *Intensive Probation and Parole: Research Findings and Policy Implications* (Santa Monica: The RAND Corporation, forthcoming).

Rosen, Cathryn Jo and Goldkamp, John S., "The Constitutionality of Drug Testing at the Bail Stage," *The Journal of Criminal Law and Criminology* (1989), 80(1): 114-176.

Schmidt, Peter and Witte, Ann Dryden, *Predicting Recidivism Using Survival Model* (New York: Springer-Verlag, 1988).

Sickmund, Melissa, Juvenile Court Drug and Alcohol Cases, 1985-1988, (Pittsburgh: National Center for Juvenile Justice, September 1990).

Stitzer, Maxine L. and McCaul, Mary E., "Criminal Justice Interventions with Drug and Alcohol Abusers: The Role of Compulsory Treatment," *Behavioral Approaches to Crime and Delinquency: A Handbook of Application, Research, and Concepts*, Morris, Edward K. and Braukmann, Curtis J., eds., New York: Plenum Press, 1987), 331-361.

Wexler, Harry K.; Falkin, Gregory P.; Lipton, Douglas S., "Outcome Evaluation of a Prison Therapeutic Community for Substance Abuse Treatment," *Criminal Justice and Behavior*, 17(1): 71-92.